"Patton and Woods hit the pause button on the constant stream of digital distractions and reintroduce the biblical concept of rest. Battle tested in classes on pop culture across many years of teaching, the authors' proposals are aimed at developing self-awareness concerning our habits of consuming digital content. For a world bombarded by advertising and awash in social media, this book is a lifeline to a welcoming haven, a manual for young and old alike in converting boredom into moments of reflection and spiritual transformation."

—**Jonathan Armstrong**, Professor of Bible and Theology, Moody Bible Institute

"I am profoundly thankful for *Everyday Sabbath*. With a deep sense of love and concern for their readers, Patton and Woods offer wise and practical advice on how to engage with media, technology, and culture in ways that are pleasing to God. Let us reclaim the *Three Sacreds*—intentionality, interiority, and identity—and put our digital world in its proper place."

—**Diane M. Badzinski**, Chair and Professor of Communication, Colorado Christian University

"Three cheers for this much-needed book! Patton and Woods faithfully help readers reclaim the Sabbath, guiding them through the choppy waters of digital dominance, screen addiction, and the constant quest for more. No judgment from these pages, only support. These two seasoned scholars remind us that the practical wisdom of the Sabbath is still within our grasp. A word in season, indeed!"

—**Stephanie Bennett**, Professor of Communication and Media Ecology, Palm Beach Atlantic University

"This is a must-read if you are seeking to mindfully use technology. This book provides scriptural and spiritual rationale for taking control of your media use to have more time each day for relationships, spiritual growth, and personal discernment. This book aims to help you develop Christ-like habits with technology, and with its scriptural references, personal reflection questions, and practical tips. It delivers!"

—**Renee Bourdeaux**, Assistant Professor of Communication Studies, Northwest University, author of *Communicating Love in Relationships*

"In encouraging the faithful to reimagine the practice of Sabbath, this book—wisely—doesn't ignore popular culture or pretend that Christians are immune to the influences of a larger society. Instead, Patton and Woods provide a path for Christians to live with intentionality in their relationship to both media and culture, becoming careful consumers of messaging while also developing spiritual practices that help mindful readers deepen their communion with God."

—**Jonathan M. Bowman**, Professor of Communication Studies,
University of San Diego

"In an age of distraction and disorientation, Patton and Woods offer timely guidance on how to resume the dance. Anyone wanting to reclaim healthy, holy habits from the domineering influences of media will appreciate this book."

—**Dennis Cali**, Distinguished Professor of Arts and Sciences,
University of Texas at Tyler

"If you are searching for an effective resource that can help you develop a deeper love and knowledge of God and fits perfectly in any small group whether in a church, a youth group, dorm-floor discussion group, or just a sacred conversation among friends, you have found it in this book. It is a resource that is easy to access and filled with ready-made questions that will help foster transformative discussions in person or by distance, as we seek to draw closer to God, so that we may become better reflections of his love to a hurting world."

—**Tom Carmody**, Professor of Communication Studies,
Vanguard University

"Just the book we need right now. *Everyday Sabbath* provides the thinking Christian with practical tools to navigate the vast ocean of technology and media in which we are immersed. In addition to offering creative exercises to help readers reflect on their media use, Patton and Woods provoke contemplation of existential questions beginning with a rich discussion of one's ultimate calling. The authors advocate stewarding the stirrings of the soul, a refreshing reminder of becoming more sensitive to life's inspirational encounters, even—and especially—on social media. A bonus is the authors' offering of a Pop Culture Shema to inspire and haunt us in discerning what is at stake in our mass-mediated choices."

—**Terri Lynn Cornwell**, Commissioned Pastor, Presbyterian Church (USA)

"This is a book that is desperately needed for these times. In a very real way, social media, technology, and streaming content threaten to enslave us and rob us of the joy of daily living. Far from advocating mere abstinence, *Everyday Sabbath* offers enormously practical and insightful guidance on how to navigate and make better (and wiser) our pop culture habits."

—**Paul A. Creasman**, Chair and Professor, Department of Communication, Arizona Christian University

"Patton and Woods tap into ancient wisdom and the eternal relevance of Scripture to brilliantly light a path forward through this contemporary co-nundrum. Spiritual shepherds and those desiring a deeper spirituality will find a humble and helpful guide in the pages of this book. So, step away from technology, take a Sabbath rest with this book, and then step right back into our digital culture to see God at work. Better yet, why not do that with others in a small group from your church? The authors have provided questions at the end of each chapter for a group of people to wrestle with together."

—**Dave Dawson**, Campus and Leadership Development Director, Bethel Church, Richland, Washington

"*Everyday Sabbath* is a much needed and a most relevant digital media literacy resource for spiritual formation. An invaluable tool, it affirms the gift of media and technology while directing us to pathways of spiritual-ity of resistance to passive consumption of digital media. Complete with how-to techniques for cultivating everyday spirituality in incremental moments, the book is a timely wake-up call to live into one's timeless vocation: love of God and care for the neighbor."

— **Glory E. Dharmaraj**, President, World Association for Christian Communication-North America

"*Everyday Sabbath* is a keystone work at a time when the need for mind-ful and sacred interaction with media and technology is greater than ever before. The authors provide a space for readers of faith to understand and use pop culture and modern communication technologies to flourish and fulfill the purpose for which they were created. Patton and Woods offer a pathway for faithfully entering rest in God's presence and becoming people involved in the work of redemption every day."

—**Denise Edwards-Neff**, Interim Dean and Professor of Communication, College of Liberal Arts and Sciences, Azusa Pacific University

"Drs. Patton and Woods provide timely counsel and advice for their readers in calling for the practice of Christian Shema: the act of intentionally listening for and therefore hearing truth from God, considering its claims and requirements, then making personal application to live within God's will and influence. This discipline stands in stark contrast to the lack of intentional hearing and living practiced, unintentionally, by the majority of twenty-first-century peoples. *Everyday Sabbath* calls Christians to take ownership of their own lives, influences, and choices, rather than allowing pop culture to influence and shape their thinking and actions."

—**Brent Ellis**, President, Spring Arbor University

"This is the book we've been waiting for! I've read numerous thoughtful works on media literacy from various perspectives—including Christian— and each one had something important to contribute to the conversation. *Everyday Sabbath*, however, gets to the heart of our interaction with pop culture and media technology. Patton and Woods share their inspired ideas in ways that are both scholarly and practical—deep and accessible. This book takes the reader on a self-reflective journey toward not only a better relationship with pop culture but a deeper relationship with God and our fellow humans. It is essential reading for anyone wanting to make the most of her high calling as a Christian in our mediated culture. We need this book, and I'm excited to share it with my colleagues and students."

—**Lynelle Ellis**, Associate Professor and Director of the Center for Media Ministry, Walla Walla University

"Patton and Woods have produced a thickly reasoned approach to surviving, even growing and prospering, in the swill of social media which, more often than we care to admit, keeps us off the dance floor pondering our place in the mediated world. *Everyday Sabbath* ranges from Augustine to Kierkegaard, Ignatius to The Simpsons, never losing sight of the key questions: Where is our ground-of-being? How do we fit in? This book should be on every teen's list, and up through the grands."

—**Mark Fackler**, Professor Emeritus, Department of Communication, Calvin University

"*Everyday Sabbath* provides a clear, accessible, and memorable look at how we can live as Christians in a media world. This book is an insightful, eye-opening, and much-needed study on what it means to be authentically and biblically literate in a technological society. If you follow the journey with these authors, your life will be transformed and you will grow closer to the One who created you."

—**Geri E. Forsberg**, Western Washington University, author of *Critical Thinking in an Image World*, and *Faculty Fellow with Faculty Commons*

"This book is a call for reclaiming the redemptive life God intends for us to live by becoming aware of our attachments to technology—attachments that often distract us from experiencing and sharing in the presence of God. This work calls us to take the time to lay our technological encumbrances aside and rest in the embrace of our Maker and the grace he provides. In so doing, we reorient our lives and rediscover the image of God within each of us. This is a practical and useful book which is timely, informed, and readable."

—**Ben Fraser**, Westminster Canterbury Fellow for Religious Studies and Lifelong Learning, Virginia Wesleyan University

"This highly readable and timely volume guides readers through a mindful assessment of (typically) unreflective social media practices, bringing Christian thinkers over the ages from Saint Augustine to C. S. Lewis into conversation with contemporary communication scholars. Integrating theory and theological reflection, popular culture references and established research findings, the authors urge us to embrace sacred intentionality, interiority, and identity through a series of practical steps, reminding us that our self-worth is found not in the number of 'Likes' and followers we have, but in our inestimable value in the eyes of a loving Creator. Outstanding!"

—**Janie M. H. Fritz**, Professor, Department of Communication and Rhetorical Studies, Duquesne University, and former president of the Religious Communication Association

"How do you navigate a world of addicting social media, untrustworthy news feeds, and polarized online opinions? With guides like Patton and Woods. In this creative book, they remind us that we are ultimately in control of our interactions with an ever-increasing digital world. They provide a practical perspective on how we might engage pop culture in ways that are rooted in biblical principles. It will encourage and challenge every Christian with a smartphone."

—**Garrett Gerhart**, Communications Director, Life Bible Fellowship Church, Upland, California

"Patton and Woods's rediscovery of the full meaning of Sabbath could not come at a more important time for our media-entranced world today. Their expert knowledge of the mediated environment coupled with a frank and humble assessment of their own journeys toward Christian mindfulness will inspire any serious reader to join in the sacred dance."

—**Andrew J. Harris**, Associate Professor of Communication, Cedarville University

"With the master metaphor of dancing, this book emulates the pattern modeled by Christ, the Lord of the Dance, who engaged human culture in a way that lovingly transformed it rather than slavishly conforming to it. Instead of prescribing do's and don'ts of media consumption, this self-described conversation-starter for the thinking Christian commends wisdom for mindful engagement with social media and pop culture. Accessible, personal, and at times poetic, Patton and Woods's writing interweaves exhortations from Scripture, insights from classic texts, findings from current research, and observations from personal experience into a timely guide to leading the dance."

—**John B. Hatch**, Professor and Chair of Communication Studies, Eastern University

"For anyone feeling lopsided in the balance of pop culture and Christian living, this is a must-read. Patton and Woods guide readers through an ever-relevant process of restoring Sabbath rhythms. This honest self-inventory will uncover habits that keep you from sacred living. It will mark the beginning of your journey to reclaim life's most valuable resource—time."

—**Vanessa Hartsell**, Founder and Executive Director of Ignite Life

"*Everyday Sabbath* is about human flourishing. Patton and Woods invite us and equip us in a technology-dominated culture to live intentionally, mindfully, redemptively, and in intensely practical, life-giving ways. *Everyday Sabbath* offers us organizing principles (holy habits) around which our lives can lead with biblical wisdom as we grapple for what will shape us the most in our dance with modern technologies. I can't think of a better book to lead us on the dance floor."

—**Gail Johnsen**, Pastor of Spiritual Formation, Faith Tri-Cities, Pasco, Washington

"Some books raise questions and some books provide answers. *Everyday Sabbath* not only does both but does so boldly and provocatively. Patton and Woods ask genuine and piercing questions and provide concrete answers that do not condemn pop culture but allow the reader to ask, who is leading whom in their pop culture dance? *Everyday Sabbath* is a must-read for every person of faith wrestling with understanding how to monitor and moderate their dance with pop culture."

—**Kevin T. Jones**, Professor of Communication Studies, George Fox University

"Patton and Woods have given the church an excellent book to help believers of all ages assess, reflect, and then act upon how they use media and technology. Before I read this book, I merely thought of Sabbath as a biblical concept that encouraged Christians to dedicate one day a week to rest and reflect upon the goodness of God. Now I see the Sabbath idea as a daily rest and a pattern of resistance to the cultural swampland bombarding me. The authors ground their ideas in substantial scholarly research in theology and communication and then do a fantastic job of intertwining them to make a powerful argument in every chapter. Each chapter has activities and questions that allow the reader to reflect and act upon important ideas and concepts. I could see this book as a useful addition for academic classes or small group study in a church focusing on media, technology, and its impact on our lives."

—**John Katsion**, Associate Professor, School of Communication and Mass Media, Northwest Missouri State University

"Patton and Woods thoughtfully discuss our spiritual dilemma in the age of technology. *Everyday Sabbath* is not just another work hammering away at the inevitable ills of social media and technology; instead, it is an invitation for spiritual reflection and sacred intentionality. It truly speaks to readers about how they might be more mindful of the spiritual dance they have with media and technology."

—**Brandon Knight**, Assistant Professor of Communication,
William Carey University

"Patton and Woods artfully offer a redemptive perspective on meaningful engagement with our media-saturated world. Their thought-provoking insights and practical applications serve as a salve for the frenetic pace of our always-on popular culture by inviting readers to re-envision their relationship with media as part of a sacred dance infused with meaning rather than a mindless trance of self-gratification. The message in this book is both profoundly relevant to our time and rich with timeless truths."

—**Alyse Lehrke**, Assistant Professor, Department of Business and
Leadership, Eastern Mennonite University

"Patton and Woods offer a modern-day primer on how to be in the world but not of the world. Perfect for a college classroom, a small group, or a personal time of reflection, their text is biblically principled and thoughtfully woven with wisdom from scholars and ancients. In addition, the personal reflection questions and discussion starters beckon us to consider and alter our daily dance with media and technology. Ultimately, Patton and Woods encourage us to be present each day."

—**Wendy Liddell**, President, Great Northern University

"Patton and Woods have opened a conversation that demands an honest response from people of faith. On the one hand, we often deplore the influence of social media upon the young while we simultaneously rely on it ourselves for everything from sermon prep to sports, and all easily justified. A great read with sobering reflection."

—**Mark McCormick**, Pastor, Mayflower Congregational Church,
Lansing, Michigan

"How can a serious Christian handle the ubiquitous presence and pull of social media and technology that swallows us whole? Patton and Woods offer a concrete vision for how to balance the constant, confusing deluge of popular culture with the need for focused discipleship. The authors shape an approach that includes Sabbath-keeping and discernment in each chapter with practical recommendations and discussions. With its accessible writing, this book is ideal for college students, small groups, and individuals. I will definitely require this timely book for my students."

—**Elizabeth W. McLaughlin**, Professor of Communication, Bethel University, Indiana, and author of *Women's Voices of Duty and Destiny*

"*Everyday Sabbath* offers a distinctively hopeful and practical guide for faithful media practices rooted in the deep wisdom of the Christian tradition from the biblical prophets to St. Augustine to C. S. Lewis. They show how disciples of Jesus may fulfill their calling to serve their neighbors and share the gospel through mindful use of and deliberate appointments with today's media platforms, while practicing Sabbath resistance to the digital trances induced by our attention-demanding devices. With eyes wide open to the deeply corrupting potential of popular culture, Patton and Woods offer a primer for holy habits by which our media consumption may be transformed into a craft of Christian service."

—**Gerald J. Mast**, Professor of Communication, Bluffton University

"*Everyday Sabbath* is a timely contribution to orthopraxy in Christian education. Patton and Woods heed the Apostle Paul's exhortation—to take captive every thought to make it obedient to Christ (2 Cor. 10:5)—and apply it to our contemporary media deluge. The authors' *Three Sacreds* heuristic calls us to reorient our identity in Christ. Critically, they do not suggest the all-too-common binary approach: avoidance of, or resignation to, a digital landscape haunted by unholy ghosts. Instead, they proffer a gospel way: Spirit-led engagement with a sin-stained world that needs Christian witness. This book will help many to rethink their viewing and sharing habits—to obey in resolution, not yield in resignation—and remind us that the Holy Ghost is greater than he who is in the machine."

—**A. Chase Mitchell**, Assistant Professor of Media and Communication, East Tennessee State University

"At a time when the pervasive influence of social media technology is at the forefront of our collective national consciousness, Patton and Woods boldly address the proverbial elephant in the room, that little voice of warning that whispers in our collective ears: are social media controlling me, or am I controlling them? Together they ask the hard questions of self-examination and provide sound biblical wisdom and insight that help us learn to lead in our dance with pop culture while walking in the light and lordship of Jesus Christ."

—**William L. Mullen**, Professor and Chair, Communication Studies Department, Shorter University

"Patton and Woods's efforts have resulted in a book that is bold and clearly passionate about spiritual formation, discernment, and media in the larger world. Yet it is also incredibly careful and well-grounded in a mature and deep understanding of both Christianity and media. This text seems ideal as a catalyst for Bible studies or book circles for teens through adults. It is also perfect as a supplemental but required text in a variety of communication courses. The issues and activities raised in this book provide readers with a toolkit for examining the single most important challenge in our personal and spiritual formation today: stewarding our engagement with media."

—**Richard K. Olsen**, Chair, Department of Communication Studies, University of North Carolina-Wilmington

"This book is fascinating! And so timely. Patton and Woods challenge readers to mindfulness in the use of media, while offering practical tools for self-reflection. The result is intentionality in consuming media in accord with one's sacred identity. *Everyday Sabbath* is ideal for pastoral ministry and small group reflection."

—**Renee Pomarico**, Communications Director, Consecrated Women of Regnum Christi

"Patton and Woods give you a plan to imitate the mind of Christ so you can experience everyday Sabbath—a life energized with renewed purpose— seeing every moment as an opportunity for serious and joy-filled play and

Sabbath rest. There are only a few books I read every year, this is now one of them. I am confident you will do the same."

—**Clint Rothell**, Associate Professor of Philosophy, Northeastern Junior College, and Statewide Discipline Chair of Philosophy, Colorado Community College System

"This is a must-read book for practically all of us. Patton and Woods have a sharp eye for both the blessings and pitfalls of our popular culture. Rather than take the easy road of high-handed condemnation and advocating retreat from the digital world, they suggest a difficult—but vital—pathway for not just surviving but thriving while surrounded by enticing screens and sound-canceling headphones. Their strong moral compass and commitment to biblical wisdom suggest that all is not lost in our entertainment-saturated culture—that we can take delight in modern creativity and art while finding space to be who God meant us to be."

—**Kevin Schut**, Professor and Chair, Department of Media and Communication, Game Development Program Lead, Trinity Western University

"As a former president of the World Association for Christian Communication, I know it's hard to learn to slurp a discerning sip from the firehose of social media. Love it or hate it, pop culture is where our world creates meaning in common. Patton and Woods propose a mindful dance with media and technology, offering a practical roadmap to help your group navigate these fecund but sometimes murky waters."

—**Dennis A. Smith**, Presbyterian Church (USA), Regional Liaison, South America (retired)

"Recognizing technology and popular culture as value-laden for both good and bad, *Everyday Sabbath* provides readers with a well-grounded faith-based guide to spiritual and practical responses to digital popular culture, leading from sacred intentionality, to sacred interiority, and sacred identity."

—**Paul A. Soukup**, S. J., Professor, Communication Department, Santa Clara University

"When it comes to the media, should we be telling people to get out of a burning building or to get onto the dance floor so we can teach them how to dance? Clearly, Patton and Woods have chosen the route of dance instructors—and they are skillful in their task. Thoughtfully and practically, they lead readers toward a more sacred curiosity, and a more Sabbath-based involvement with the media. I was inspired!"

—**Gregory Spencer**, Professor of Communication Studies, Westmont College, author of *Awakening the Quieter Virtues and Reframing the Soul*

"Everyday Sabbath reminds readers of their malformed relationship with pop culture derived from fear, anxiety, or existential boredom. Situating ancient wisdom within a contemporary context, Patton and Woods encourage readers to realign their relationship with pop culture through the sacred disciplines of Sabbath rest."

—**Jeffrey Tabone**, Assistant Professor of Humanities, Assistant Director of the John Wesley Honors College, Indiana Wesleyan University

"Living in a world of continual innovation and unpredictable circumstances all but guarantees the role of technology and media in our everyday lives is likely to continue growing. Patton and Woods have laid out wise principles and signposts marking out a path of faithful stewardship and balance that can be followed regardless of what our future holds."

—**Troy Tabor**, Cambodia Media Ministry Director, Assemblies of God World Missions

"Artfully weaving Scripture, scholarship from theology and media, experience, and popular culture, *Everyday Sabbath* represents a countercultural work. The book drew me to personal reflection and transcendent truths from Scripture to consider my own media consumption and its influence on my spiritual, academic, psychological, and physical well-being."

—**R. Tyler Spradley**, Associate Professor of Communication, Stephen F. Austin State University

"Patton and Woods uncover fresh spiritual disciplines focused on intentionality, interiority, and identity and use them to counter today's cultural anxieties—anxieties exacerbated by our media use. Shaped by Scripture, their cultural dance metaphor leaps with energy and lands solidly on the ground with practical applications in every chapter."

—**Annalee Ward**, Director, Wendt Character Initiative, University of Dubuque

"*Everyday Sabbath* emphasizes living like Christ but not according to the whims of those who post emotionally destructive missives. By entering the dance with Jesus, readers will be equipped to transform their personal lives and ensure the future of a stronger Christian witness. I highly recommend that you dance along with Patton and Woods."

—**Ken Waters**, Professor of Journalism, Pepperdine University

"Patton and Woods offer a series of reflective and practical comebacks to a culture obsessed with lethal efficiency and infinite entertainment. Reflective and pragmatic, the authors stretch the imagination and teach the soul to sidestep the shallow culture of entertainment and efficiency and launch out into deeper waters. Patton and Woods give us a directed meditation on the poisons of efficiency and distraction that have become the definition of our culture, and they offer a grounded response to those toxins."

—**Mark Williams**, Professor of Rhetoric,
California State University, Sacramento

"Instead of writing a book that shames those of us who spend a lot of time with popular culture, Patton and Woods rightly refocus our attention on the spirituality of our lifetime journey. Our engagement with popular culture demands an attentiveness to the most mundane parts of our daily lives—waking up, remembering, confessing, and attending to our emotions. These aren't just good habits, they are spiritual practices that enable us to resist the damaging social hierarchies that pervade our lives and our institutions. They are spiritual practices that enable us to heal."

—**Naaman Wood**, Associate Professor of Media and Communication Studies, Redeemer University

Everyday Sabbath

Everyday Sabbath

How to Lead Your Dance with Media and Technology
in Mindful and Sacred Ways

PAUL D. PATTON *and*
ROBERT H. WOODS JR.

FOREWORD BY Nathan Foster
PREFACE BY Al Kresta

CASCADE *Books* · Eugene, Oregon

EVERYDAY SABBATH
How to Lead Your Dance with Media and Technology in Mindful and Sacred Ways

Cascade Books
An Imprint of Wipf and Stock Publishers
199 W. 8th Ave., Suite 3
Eugene, OR 97401

www.wipfandstock.com

PAPERBACK ISBN: 978-1-7252-7277-4
HARDCOVER ISBN: 978-1-7252-7276-7
EBOOK ISBN: 978-1-7252-7278-1

Cataloguing-in-Publication data:

Names: Patton, Paul D., 1952–. | Woods, Robert H., Jr., 1970–.

Title: Everyday sabbath : how to lead your dance with media and technology in mindful and sacred ways / Paul D. Patton and Robert H. Woods, Jr.

Description: Eugene, OR: Cascade Books, 2021 | Includes bibliographical references and index.

Identifiers: ISBN 978-1-7252-7277-4 (paperback) | ISBN 978-1-7252-7276-7 (hardcover) | ISBN 978-1-7252-7278-1 (ebook)

Subjects: LCSH: Social media—Religious aspects—Christianity. | Mass media—Religious aspects—Christianity. | Popular culture—Religious aspects—Christianity.

Classification: P94 .E96 2021 (print) | P94 (ebook)

Dedication

To our friend, colleague, copyeditor, and dear sister in Christ, Marsha Daigle-Williamson (1946–2020). You will be missed, deeply. Thank you for always "speaking the truth in love" (Eph. 4:15, NIV). Your work on this book, and others, will never be forgotten.—Paul and Robert

To my grandchildren (in chronological order): Caleb Rock, Logan Justice, Micah Blaze, Miles Dean, Bennett David, Arlo Patton, and Monroe Grace. My prayer, and often my plea, is that you would find the wisdom to transcend the dominant motifs of the world, categorized in Saint John's first epistle (2:16, KJV) as "the lust of the eyes" [consumerism], "the lust of the flesh" [sensualism], and the "pride of life" [egoism]. That you would love deeply, think wisely, and forgive quickly. And to the Reverend John Peck, a pastoral mentor whose life and wisdom still hovers with great grace.—Paul

To my wife and best friend, Rebekah, who gives me space to explore the unknown; to my mother, Margareta, who encouraged me to ask questions and pursue education; to my father, Bob (1935–2020), who taught me discipline; to my sister-in-law, Tabitha, who reminded me to be a voice for the voiceless; to my sister, Audrey, who challenged me to keep it real; and above all, to my Lord and Savior Jesus Christ for his matchless grace. Pax Christi.—Robert

Table of Contents

TABLE OF CONTENTS

Foreword

GOD IS AN INFINITE BEING who likes to create.

Wonderful things.

Beautiful things.

Helpful things.

Things that bear a mark of beauty, truth, and goodness.

It only takes a brief pause, a few moments of intentionally noticing the natural world around us, the one just outside our door, and we quickly uncover an abounding expanse of brilliance, harmony, and creative wonder.

With prayerful curiosity we might just conclude there is a sense of play, joy, and delight in God's crafting and sustaining of our world.

Why hide delicately clothed flowers in a mountain meadow? Why do little birds chirping and singing bring us a sense of delight? Is it necessary for the roaring river carving canyons and cascading off cliffs to inspire in us a sense of majesty?

Or the sun, joining a chorus of planets, quietly dancing though our solar system offering latent lessons on the cycle of life and death?

We are surrounded by a complex tapestry of self-sustaining systems linked through harmonious movement, all instinctively doing what they are designed to do—obey the will of the Father.

And of course, within the vastness of our galaxy, earth is little more than a grain of sand. It is impossible to even begin to imagine the creative wonders the Trinity has been crafting through the ages in the vastness of some two trillion other galaxies.

God is an infinite being who likes to create.

And then here we are, the crowning jewel of God's creative endeavors on earth. Beloved, handcrafted, eternal beings woven together in God's image, encapsulated in bodies with regenerative systems so detailed and intricate that our best efforts can barely grasp them.

In some strange and wonderful sense, we bear the thumbprint of the Creator of the galaxies. By thoughtfully and carefully arranging the raw materials God has buried, planted, and scattered around our planet, we too create.

Wonderful things.

Beautiful things.

Helpful things.

Things that bear a mark of beauty, truth, and goodness.

These realities culminate into one very simplistic and critical point: Human creation holds the potential to be a wonderful gift from God for the betterment of humanity. The technological advances and media and technology that dominate and define much of our waking life have come to us as the product of something good and therefore God-inspired.

It is not difficult to find a glimmer of the beauty and goodness of God in the many wonders humans construct. Art, film, music, medicine, architecture, and technology all have the potential to naturally bear the mark of the Creator who crafted us.

Within the biblical narrative we find over and over again God's relentless desire to engage in human affairs. Not only does God seem to delight in helping, inspiring, and guiding humans in our creative endeavors, but throughout history God continues to unlock the vast potential and possibilities of the raw treasures and resources our planet holds. God creates with us.

Of course, not all human creations are good—far from it. While we live within the possibility to co-labor with God to bring great good upon the earth, we also possess an innate propensity for destruction, and our labors may result in nothing more than shrines to human depravity.

By its very nature, evil cannot create; evil can only twist, distort, and corrupt that which was already good. The hallmarks are always the same; systems and mechanisms rooted in selfishness and power. When we curve inward, it always leads to the dehumanization of other image bearers and ultimately ourselves—media and technology are not immune.

What we as a species now face in terms of access to entertainment, communication, and information is completely unprecedented in the whole of human existence.

The searing rate at which we have been thrust into this new way of living has outpaced our capacity to help one another engage in these new media with wisdom and health.

We are now presented with unparalleled challenges to live free from the intoxicating and crushing pull to comparison. It is almost as if the cultural default is to center our lives and joys around an insatiable desire for more information, gossip, and mind-numbing entertainment, all at the cost of being truly present to those near and dear.

The myriad of new platforms in which to engage with the world leaves many of us empty and unfulfilled. Evil has twisted our healthy and valid human longings to be seen, connected, and accepted with other image bearers. This, in part, may explain the exponential rise in loneliness, anxiety, and depression we as a species are now facing.

Our society is desperately lacking the tools and resources to use new innovations for the long-term good of humanity, to live in this world as free beings rather than victims of an insatiable machine hell-bent on more.

More "Likes."

More information.

More scrolling.

What you will find in the pages of this book are invaluable insights and practical tools to help us navigate the amazing, and potentially treacherous, expanse of pop culture.

This may be the most important modern book you read.

As you begin working with this text, I would like to offer a few thoughts I think you will find helpful.

I encourage you to approach this work with an openness and sense of discovery and adventure. Being willing to critically look at the cultural soup we have been swimming in, as well as our consumption habits, requires a certain level of honesty, strength, and even courage. I am certain that if you thoughtfully and honestly work with this text then what you will learn about yourself and the world around you will serve you well for years to come.

Know that this is not a book about disconnecting from the world or suffering for the sake of some misguided religious conviction. This is a book about freedom and growing in awareness of how our habits of consumption influence and affect us, both good and bad. My hope is that you will befriend this work with a prayerful and playful posture, allowing God to teach and guide you into a deeper movement towards fullness of heart and life.

One of the great strengths of this book is the array of practices it offers. Both authors have spent years teaching and honing these exercises. As their academic colleague, I repeatedly witnessed genuine transformation in the lives of countless students who seriously worked with these practices.

At first glance some of these practices may seem difficult or monotonous. You will do well to look beyond the potential discomfort you may experience and view them as an invitation to experiment and locate a window into a deeper life with God.

One word of caution: Do not let a sense of perfectionism get in the way of your work with the exercises. The point is to learn and be with God. Obsessing about your performance will potentially cheat you out of the good they have to offer.

As you embark on your journey through this book, know you are in good hands. Paul and Robert are trusted guides. I have immense respect for their expertise and the genuineness in which they seek health in their own dance with pop culture.

Have fun.

Nathan Foster
Renovaré
Author of *The Making of an Ordinary Saint*

Preface

FOR A GENERATION, Paul Patton and Robert Woods have enjoyed the fascinating vantage point of working as professors of communication at Spring Arbor University. Every day they have taught students to think critically about the ever-expanding environment of pop culture in which students, and increasingly, all of us, live, move, and have our being. Both men have engaged the issues surrounding modern media and popular culture at both the theoretical and practical levels. They have also co-authored a Christian introduction to media criticism titled *Prophetically Incorrect*. Patton is also an accomplished playwright, theater director, and performer. Woods has also coauthored *Media Ethics: Cases and Moral Reasoning* and co-edited *Understanding Evangelical Media*, to which Patton is a contributing author. Both have observed and participated in the perpetually changing and roiling world of communications technology, media content, and the processes and practices of Hollywood, Madison Avenue, and Silicon Valley. They do not just critique pop culture but create and consume it.

Mass media usually refer to a one-way stream of communication from producer to audience. Social media, in contrast, refer to two-way or interactive media. Similarly, professors Patton and Woods have not only taught one-way from podium to class, but they have also benefited from two-way communication: They learn, and so we learn, from their students who are principal consumers of pop culture. This book overflows with insight gained from understanding how students use media, create media content, and parcel out their allotted daily twenty-four hours in consumption of media. They not only *describe* the new challenges, but they also *prescribe* what students and all of us must know to be technologically literate and faithful disciples in our use, creation, and sharing of mass and social media.

Patton and Woods have a clear understanding of media history and criticism since World War II. Most everyone knows that media content changes constantly. Talk all you want about the Golden Days of Television, Classic Films or *Rolling Stones'* Top 500 Albums of All Time, but those lists will be revised next year and audiences will inevitably move on to newer, more novel productions. Patton and Woods are not only acutely aware of changes in media content and production standards, they also know that each generation finds itself shaped by the different technologies that deliver content. "We shape our tools, and thereafter our tools shape us" taught the patron saint of media studies, Marshall McLuhan. Patton and Woods have lived through and watched the Baby Boomers enter the shallow waters of pop culture in magazines, billboards, portable transistor radios, 45 rpm records, rock festivals, and family-centered television. The tide continued to rise with GenXers and millennials who were quickly awash in a stream of Internet flotsam including new forms of marketing, buying, selling, gaming, entertaining, and content liberated from the moral boundaries of the Hollywood production code.

Today's iGens are swimming, often drowning, in an unending torrent of social media delivered over innumerable platforms and gushing from hand-held devices that promise instant information, gratification, and communion. You can now view a *One Direction* music video, add your own comments to a list beneath the screen, and send it to your brother; listen to an interview with the Saudi executioner including video footage of a beheading; locate a tutorial on how to carve a walking stick; add "fix broken faucet" to your "to do" list; identify a meadowlark that just landed in the field just east of you; take a snapshot of your privates and send a sexting message to buddies or bonnies; complain about your fourth-hour teacher on Instagram; purchase tickets to a Detroit Tigers game; and pray the Rosary one right after the other as you sit in a traffic jam on I-94 towards Chicago, cursing that you did not consult the red lines on your Google map app. Our smartphones are so integrated into our comings and goings, our risings and our retirings, that they resemble prostheses, and are held every bit as necessary and dear. Woe to the one who comes between an adolescent and his smartphone.

Unfortunately, many have stopped listening to the warnings about the unintended negative consequences of the indiscriminate use of modern technology and pop culture. Critics are caricatured as Luddites or as suffering from apocalyptic fever. So, we have all heard about addictive technology and how we can amuse ourselves to death like caged rats hitting the reward button until their brains are fried from the pleasant electric sensation delivered. And like those whose houses are sitting on the San Andreas Fault, we console ourselves that earthquakes happen to other people. So, let me probe: Is there anyone reading this page who has not felt his occasional powerlessness to stop checking his email? Or felt an inability to cease surfing from page to obliquely related page on the Internet while trivial curiosity tempts him to keep googling one tangentially related topic after another? And how about games from video poker to Xbox? I know a man ashamed that he once missed a day of work because he was so fix-ated on getting to the final, fifteenth level of a video game. Me, the man. "Heretic," the game. Have you never felt the obsession of tallying Instagram or Facebook "Likes"? Have you never felt insecure or worried when your friend, lover, co-worker, husband, or daughter took longer to respond to your last text message or tweet than you thought was necessary? Who has not vainly watched good conversation time squandered because someone at the dinner table is sharing something hilarious? YouTube videos of toddlers chortling, cats on trapezes, army recruiters rapping some enlistment rag, or newscasters speaking the unspeakable because they forgot the microphone was hot? On another occasion, each video might have been a launching pad for worthy conversation, but the parade of them one after another keeps us laughing and just rolling forward to the next one. Our discourse is limited to "Crazy," "Unbelievable," "Have you ever seen anything like that?" "How does he do that?" "Can you say that on the air?" "Gee Whiz."

It is not just the wasted time that comes from indiscriminate and mindless consumption of pop culture; there is often a psychological mar-ring, an abuse of soul that occurs. In the social media world, "know thyself" is replaced with "show and maintain thyself." One of Patton and Woods's students was becoming more aware of herself in light of her online self. She was confused. "When others criticize or dislike what I post, it lowers my self-worth. I become ashamed of who I am. But when my messages are liked—even loved—by others, I feel good about myself and like my quirky personality. Am I losing sight of myself? I can feel confident in myself one moment and then disgusted with myself the next. I know this is not healthy, but I am pretty sure I am not the only one who feels this way... or at least I hope not!!!???" (p. 102).

She is not. Yet social networking can provide healthy and meaningful interactions. Family and friends can share more regular updates, videos, and photos to the benefit and blessing of all. But for many, "Likes" and re-tweets received can become quantifiable affirmation of their ascending relational significance in a hierarchy of friends, colleagues, and followers. In our efforts to garner attention and approval we slowly manipulate our persona, secretly wondering if the real self is truly worthy enough to be liked by anyone or generate more than just a few "Likes." Ironically, in shaping our identity to conform to what others find acceptable we relinquish the very uniqueness we should cherish.

Besides the wasting of time and the malforming of ourselves, we may also form an electronic cocoon from which we are reluctant to emerge. It protects and panders. We form a social and entertainment culture by weaving a fabric of our favorite bloggers, YouTube sites, Hulu channels, conversation forums, and live within this world adapted to our tastes and interests. Recent studies indicate a lowering of teen promiscuity. Social conservatives initially welcomed the news until it was pointed out that lowering of promiscuity was not because the virtue of chastity had been revived. Rather, many young men felt that dating was too much of a hassle. Their social life is conveniently handled online which requires less transparency or vulnerability than actual face-to-face relationships. Are adolescents really saying, "Why date, when we can message and send pictures?" Or is the libido of young men no longer driving them to impress young women because they maintain a fantasy life online with more or less pornographic images? I find it hard to accept that the end of this trend resembles the 2013 creepy movie, *Her*, in which a heartbroken writer played by Joaquin Phoenix develops a loving, erotic relationship with a computer operating system, a sensitive entity named "Samantha" played by Scarlett Johansen. But there is significant research that indiscriminate immersion in the electronic non-stop stream of information and entertainment choices can affect mental health, lower self-esteem, and diminish happiness.

To their credit, Patton and Woods are not scared off by such developments. They see the formation of pop culture and the technologies that create and deliver it as fundamentally good. In the beginning, humans were called to cultivate the created world. The great scientific enterprise that has its roots in the late middle ages and begins to flower in the sixteenth century is originally an overflow of Christian thought and practice. Out of the scientific enterprise, technologies develop to help overcome some of the negative consequences of the Fall and to positively enable humans to create culture. That continues today as we look at the flourishing of medical and communications technologies and even the development of artificial intelligence. However, all that humans create and steward should serve the common good of human flourishing. That includes our entertainment choices. Ultimately, all that we create stands under God's just judgment. Does it serve the good of human flourishing? Or does it contribute to human debasement? To discern the difference, we must cultivate wisdom. To strengthen their point, Patton and Woods quote Pope Francis's message on the Fiftieth World Communications Day, January 24, 2016. He teaches that modern technology is "a gift of God which involves a great responsibility . . . It is not technology which determines whether or not communication is authentic, but rather the human heart and our capacity to use wisely the means at our disposal" (p. 8).

Why are we here? For what were we created? Or as Wendell Berry asked, "What are people for?" The Apostle Paul believed the end of human existence required a radical change in ourselves: "Do not lie to one another, seeing that you have put off the old nature with its practices and have put on the new nature, which is being renewed in knowledge after the image of its creator" (Col. 3:9–10, RSV). He describes this as an ongoing transformation in Christ: "And we all, with unveiled face, beholding the glory of the Lord, are being changed into his likeness from one degree of glory to another; for this comes from the Lord who is the Spirit" (2 Cor. 3:18, RSV). We become what we behold: "Beloved, we are God's children now; it does not yet appear what we shall be, but we know that when he appears we shall be like him, for we shall see him as he is" (1 John 3:2, RSV). The power of our attention to shape our sense of self runs throughout biblical and Christian spirituality. What arrests our attention becomes part of us. A culture of digital noise, constant distraction, and perpetual entertainment poses definite challenges but the human task remains the same: We are made for God.

So how can men and women of good will properly understand and use pop culture and modern communications technology to flourish and fulfill the purpose for which they were created? Patton and Woods use the metaphor of the dance partner. Pop culture stands by, always seeking to arrest our attention, always beckoning us to dance. And, inevitably, all will dance to a greater or lesser degree because there is no escaping the world of pop culture. Just consider the ubiquity of modern advertising, not to mention streaming music, videos, satellite radio, handheld television, feature films, and television monitors plastered all over restaurant walls. When he wrote for *Advertising Age*, Bob Garfield lamented,

> You cannot walk down the street without being bombarded. . . .
> You stand in an elevator looking at advertising in the corner of the

elevator car. And you go to play golf and you go to pick the ball up out of the cup, and there's an ad in the bottom of it. And you look up at the sky, and there's skywriting. And you look at a bus passing, and there's advertising. And you walk in Times Square and you go, "Is this Las Vegas on the Hudson? Am I entrapped inside a pinball machine?"[1]

Our dance partner is always beckoning. The question is, who will lead? To catch a break, Patton and Woods prescribe rediscovering the biblical idea of Sabbath rest.

Sabbath rest goes beyond setting aside a day of the week in which one rests from all servile labor. Our Creator desires that our daily existence be marked by freeing, energizing rest and alertness. Sabbath offers resistance against the chronic consumerism that lays down and surrenders to every entertainment impulse and technological option surrounding us. Sabbath rest fortifies us so our attention is freed from the tyranny of the now and not easily "fragmented by the 24/7 bombardment of pop cultural delights competing for our loyalties and passions" (p. 11).

To help us focus on what it means to develop an ongoing Sabbath rest in our daily life, Patton and Woods quote Rabbi Abraham Joshua Heschel, "There is something sacred in every moment." The squandering of our time in mindless pop cultural pursuits belittles a divine gift: our time. They develop three key constructs that make us more aware of the sacred moment and mindful pop culture engagement:

1. *Sacred Intentionality*, which connects our use of pop culture with life's overarching purpose.

2. *Sacred Interiority*, which develops the power to discern the value and effect of pop culture productions.

3. *Sacred Identity*, which distinguishes our divinely created personhood from the external self that dominates social media and celebrity culture.

These *Three Sacreds* together form a spiritual discipline for a new technological era. They enable us to develop a biblically informed mindfulness with our pop culture dance partner. Cultivating them, our authors note, helps us from "dancing in a trance" and settles the question of who takes the lead. By developing a "holy habit" of alertness to the presence, power, and provision of God in every sacred moment, we submit our entertainment desires to God's reality and his kingdom priorities.

It is high time to develop technological and media literacy if we are to receive the blessing God intends from the remarkable and unprecedented productions now accessible to us through modern communications technologies. I have yet to read a better, more cogent, more aware, more pastorally-oriented approach to dealing with the ever-present and ever-beckoning dance partner of popular culture. For anyone wondering how to draw the right boundaries of time and content, how to discern the good, the true, and the beautiful in today's popular culture and how to integrate one's spirituality with the innumerable choices now available to us in the worlds of entertainment, social communications, news and information, this book not only bears reading, it bears practicing and then lots of tweeting and re-tweeting.

Al Kresta
President and CEO of Ave Maria Radio
Host of "Kresta in the Afternoon"

Acknowledgments

WE OWE A DEBT of gratitude to many individuals and groups of people for supporting us during this process and offering feedback that helped us to serve our primary audience better.

Friends and colleagues like Ronnie Ferguson, Laura Lee Groves, Beth Patton, Tabitha Anderson, and Gail Johnsen read drafts of this book and offered invaluable feedback. Clint Rothell challenged us to be clearer with the dance metaphor, and it was Clint who likened the "trance dance" (in chapter 2) to grocery shopping without a shopping list. Rich Lewthwaite pressed us about the hierarchical insecurities related to feeling insulted that appear in chapters 7 and 8. David Thorne helped us to see through younger, wiser eyes. Steve Patton (1949–2021) generously stood with us, disagreeing at times. Finally, thanks to Jen Letherer—who should be president. Jen saw from the beginning the importance of the dance and encouraged us to press on. Thank you, one and all.

A special thanks to our hundreds of former "Intro to Pop Culture" students who for the last fifteen years at Spring Arbor University shared stories, struggles, and solutions in their dance with media, technology, and culture. We asked you to review the material in this book and make it more accessible and compelling and able to stand the test of time. Your stories fill these pages. Your input made our work much better than it would have been otherwise.

An enormous thanks to Marsha Daigle Williamson (1946–2020) who served as our primary copyeditor on this project. Marsha went home to be with her heavenly Father shortly before this book was published. She was one of the wisest people we knew. Marsha was an exceptional editor who provided far more than basic copyediting skills. She brought an in-depth understanding of Christian history and theology and languages. She had a keen nose for sniffing out what stunk and knew how to make it better. She loved clarity and pushed us to serve our readers better. That Marsha was a five-time teacher-of-the-year award winner meant that we worked under the umbrella of accountability and no small amount of fear and trembling at times. Everyone needs a Marsha. She will be missed.

Spring Arbor University's library staff (Elizabeth Walker-Papke, Karen Parsons, Kami Moyer, Susan Panak, and Robbie Bolton) provided research support that allowed us to stay on schedule. They tracked down quotes and sources that we could not. Like other librarians, they are the unsung heroes of the publishing world.

Former student Kayla Williamson, now a thriving content creator in New York, designed the graphics and layout of this book (www. kayla-williamson.com).

We are grateful for Cascade Book editors like Rodney Clapp, whom we worked with on another book more than a decade ago. We are thankful to Rodney, Matthew Wimer, and others at Cascade Books who recognized the significance of this project.

Finally, we are extremely grateful for our spouses, Beth Patton and Rebekah Woods, on many fronts. For their patience in hearing us read random paragraphs. For their insights in spiritual direction and care. And for introducing us to some of their favorite spiritual guides. Their wisdom helped us all along the way. They are constant sources of joy and refreshment.

As with all projects we undertake, we absolve all our friends and colleagues of any responsibility for any weaknesses that remain.

An Opening Note to Our Readers

THANK YOU FOR TAKING time to interact with the ideas presented in this book. Whether you were required to read this book for a class or small group, accepted a recommendation from a friend, or just found it laying around and decided to give it a try, we are grateful for your presence. As fans of good books, we tried to bring the best of our favorite reads to this project so you might feel engaged, challenged, and even inspired no matter where you might find yourself. Before you begin, we want to provide you with a few road signs to help mark your journey.

A Pre- and Post-Pandemic Project

When we started this book, it was pre-pandemic life and times. Much has changed since we first sat together in a local Michigan diner to hash out the contents of this book. Little did we know that this book's central arguments and relevance would come to life before us in some kind of twisted and unplanned experiment that would put our claims and practices to the test.

Thanks to COVID-19, we were blessed—or cursed—with more discretionary time than ever, left to our own devices, at home for hours upon hours, forced to figure out how to use the most amount of down-time we have ever experienced in our lives. We had more free time than ever before to fill with mass-mediated offerings and social media exchanges that contributed to both meaningfulness and meaning-lessness. More boredom. More emotional and cognitive agitation; fear of the unknown and frustration over the unsettled; anger over the lack of certainty about national stability, community, family, and personal health.

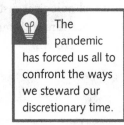

The pandemic has forced us all to confront the ways we steward our discretionary time.

The screens on all our devices pulsated their balm-like capacities. The days started blurring into weeks and then months and if we were fortunate enough to avoid or survive the virus, we were frustrated by our need to keep up with the news cycle that seemed to turn over several times each hour. For many, it was harder to hear the Savior pronouncing his constant invitation, "Come to me, all you who are weary and burdened, and I will give you rest" (Matt. 11: 28, NIV).

Meanwhile, churches faced their own set of unique challenges. Many had to quickly pivot to online delivery, which raised important questions like "What is the real nature of the church?" "What does it mean to gather as the Body?" "What content should we deliver and how often?" and "How do we continue to help our people grow spiritually through technology?" Pastors rented space in the churches of Google and Facebook, immersed in a universe of "Likes" and "Shares," not recognizing fully that inhabiting those technological spaces came with price tags on the very spiritual formation they were seeking to encourage.

So, as you read, note that everything below was written prior to COVID-19 but, we suggest, has become more relevant, more urgent, more impactful, than in pre-COVID-19 times. Please do some comparison before and after the pandemic to settle in on how your relationship with media and technology has changed during these times. We believe this additional reflective work will add value to your reading experience and bring about positive changes in your journey of lifelong learning.

Our Central Arguments

At no time in modern media history have the number and type of media and technological distractions been so readily accessible. Such distractions interfere with our ability to experience solitude, rest, Sabbath, and spiritual growth.

 FULL-TIME DISTRACTION

"Everyone is distracted. All the time."[1]

—Justin Rosenstein, the Facebook engineer who created the "Like" button

In a nutshell, we argue that the biblical notion of Sabbath is under a unique kind of assault in our digital culture. Our technological culture assumes that human beings are simply too inefficient, too inconsistent, and too lacking in processing speed to judge or solve our greatest societal problems accurately. As human beings are devalued and technological processes elevated to God-like status, key biblical concepts like community, solitude, and sabbath get distorted. Rather than think of human beings as made in the image or likeness of God (Gen. 1:26–28), we come to think of the ideal person as one who is made in the perfect image of Silicon Valley's digital likeness. In other words, the more like a machine you are in thought and deed, the better human being you become (so says our digital culture). This digital way of thinking, or worldview, invades every aspect of our lives: home, work, and church. It changes the way we think about God, ourselves, our neighbors, and the environment. No one is immune from its effects.

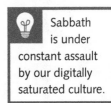

Sabbath is under constant assault by our digitally saturated culture.

Biblical sabbath is not just about whether someone can work or shop on Sunday. Instead, it is about faithfully entering God's perpetual rest and becoming a person involved in the work of redemption each day. Over time, however, our 24/7 digital flood of distractions can drown out our capacity to find rest in God's presence. Sabbath rest in a digital culture depends on the experience and cultivation of three core elements that are constantly under attack: (1) sacred *intentionality*, or a purposefulness toward God's ultimate calling; (2) sacred *interiority*, or an immediately accessible inner thought life and memory serving redemptive purposes; and (3) sacred *identity*, or an understanding of who we are and who we are to become as people made in the image of God. We call these the *Three Sacreds*.

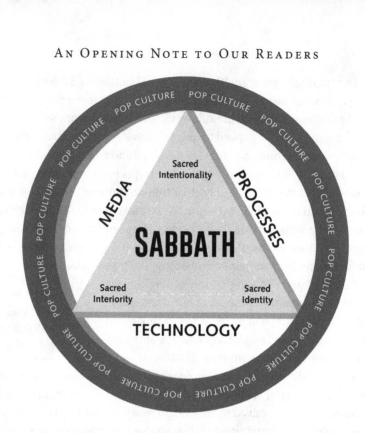

Restoring Sabbath in a digital culture begins not by condemning God's great gifts of media and technology but by approaching them with *sacred mindfulness*. Mindfulness has become a trendy, worn-out expression in many circles. But a Christian understanding of mindfulness is rooted in biblical tradition and is a timeless tool that is useful for instruction in all areas of life. The kind of mindfulness we are proposing begins with an understanding of how the technology we use every day uses and changes us in unanticipated ways. It then moves to an understanding of certain "holy habits" we can regularly practice to help confront our digital culture's dominant worldview. If people regularly practice the *Three Sacreds* above, we suggest that it is possible to experience *everyday Sabbath* in one's relationship with media and technology without merely unplugging or detaching on a single day like Sunday.

> Restoring Sabbath begins with sacred mindfulness and holy habits.

In a technological age, Christians are called to be "resistance fighters" who take part in worldview guerilla warfare and practice what Christian apologist and author C. S. Lewis describes as "resistance thinking" in our daily involvement with media and technology.[2] Given the unique characteristics of technology, resistance fighters must be equipped with equally unique tools like the *Three Sacreds*.

Some Key Assumptions

We assume that many of you, like your authors, are wearied at some level by the non-stop stream of information and entertainment choices at your fingertips. You probably check your devices more often than you like—and at inappropriate times—and may even experience "phantom vibrations." You undoubtedly find at times that the daily pressure to keep up with newsfeeds and messaging robs you of solitude and sidetracks you from other soul-nourishing communication you desire with God, yourself, and neighbors. Some of you may even be familiar with the research we share throughout this book that highlights the negative effects of media and technology on self-esteem, happiness, and mental health.

> How can I faithfully engage media and technology in mindful ways that promote everyday Sabbath and witness Christ's love to the world?

And we suspect that many of you, like your authors, may be interested in questions such as "Given the minor and sometimes major negative effects of media and technology on my life, how can I experience *everyday* Sabbath rest in ways that cultivate spiritual growth and neighborly love as I seek to be a Christ-like witness?" Or, "How can I faithfully engage media and technology in mindful ways that help promote the presence of God's peace and justice to a hurting world?" Enter this book.

How to Use This Book

We wrote this book for the "thinking Christian" who wants to develop a biblically based, holistic way to respond to our digital culture's worldview and grow Christ-like habits of the high-tech heart. The book's practical tips, exercises, and discussion questions make it ideal for personal or small group study in churches. It may also be used as a companion text for courses in pop culture, media and technology, and spiritual formation. Deep gazers will be drawn to the private conversations and commentary with the authors in each chapter's endnotes. Embedded quotes, reflections, and research notes break up long pages of text while providing additional reflection for interested readers. We encourage you to get wrapped up in a breakout box for days, even weeks, treating certain quotes or reflections as mini devotionals. You will encounter several different breakouts marked by the following icons:

Scripture	*Reflective Question*
Key Term or Idea	*Important Quote*
Relevant Research	*Practical Tip*

Our Approach

Our students over the last decade encouraged us to write this book to extend our classroom discussion with family and friends. Their testimonies of personal transformation compelled us to take the plunge. We wrote this book primarily for Christian audiences but it will appeal to a more general religious audience seeking to redeem discretionary time and live faithfully in a digitally dominated age.

We do not pretend to walk continually in mindful media wisdom. Any mini-sermons you encounter likely began as sermons we preached to ourselves in response to our own addictive binges. And to make sure we communicated our ideas as clearly as possible, we sought feedback from future readers. We looked for examples with staying power and clung to those that invited the fullness of Christian expression in both Protestant and Catholic traditions. We followed up abstract propositions with every-day examples. In final analysis, we tried to wed ourselves to good ideas and not our own preferences for self-expression.

To maintain a singular voice throughout we used "we" and "our" with most examples to avoid the tedium of parsing out our individual experiences. We figured you would not care too much whose example it was as long as it was a good one.

Finally, some books are conversation starters on a topic while others are fuller scholarly treatments spanning several hundred pages and dozens of footnotes per chapter. This book clearly fits the former category while pointing you to the latter and should be evaluated accordingly. The scholarly works that  form the basis of our arguments are identified in our endnotes, and we regularly point out their nuances in relation to our ongoing arguments throughout the book.

With gratitude,

Paul D. Patton / Spring Arbor, MI
Robert H. Woods Jr. / Pasco, WA

INTRODUCTION
AND BACKGROUND

Chapter 1

Dancing in the Dark
(Boring Ourselves to Death)

"The only thing that consoles us for our miseries is diversion [distraction]. And yet it is the greatest of our miseries. For it is that above all which prevents us thinking about ourselves and leads us imperceptibly to destruction. But for that we should be bored, and boredom would drive us to seek more solid means of escape, but diversion [distraction] passes our time and brings us imperceptibly to death."[1]

—BLAISE PASCAL, SEVENTEENTH-CENTURY FRENCH
MATHEMATICIAN AND CATHOLIC THEOLOGIAN

"The last enemy to be destroyed is death."

—1 CORINTHIANS 15:26 (NIV)

THIS BOOK'S SEEDS WERE planted one sunny fall afternoon through nearly identical experiences, years before your authors ever met. On that fateful Sunday, shortly after we returned home from church in our respective states, each of us grabbed some lunch, headed for the recliner, and spent nearly nine hours watching three successive NFL football games.

When the last whistle blew we turned off the television and sat alone in the quiet dark. For some this might sound like an ideal day. But as we surveyed the open chip bags and candy wrappers we felt exhausted and

3

depressed. The clocks on the wall mocked us. Nine hours of life were gone forever because we decided that there was nothing better to do that afternoon. Sadly, this was not the first experience of this kind for either of us. Maybe you can relate?

NAME YOUR DISTRACTION

Binge-watching your favorite program. A social media marathon session that started innocently with a funny cat video and ended four hours later with you posting forty photos of your latest vacation. Or an online competitive bargain shopping experience that lasted three hours. What is it for you?

The next morning, in a heightened flash of self-awareness, we each had a "come to Jesus" moment where we decided to find better things to do with our discretionary time; to move away from the "spectator passivity" that had incrementally and insidiously dominated our lives.[2] We recognized ourselves in Jesus's parable as the "workers in the vineyard," standing around all day doing nothing because "no one has hired us" (Matt. 20:6, 7, NIV). We understood our football binge as a symptom of a more serious underlying disease called *boredom*.[3]

We are not suggesting that boredom in and of itself is inherently sinful or without benefit;[4] rather, boredom left to its own selfish, purposeless devices often results in listless living and poor stewardship of time and talents. In other words, we can literally bore ourselves to death—death of purpose, identity, and kingdom service. In our own lives, we realized that instead of redeeming our downtime to spark creativity, meaningful reflection, or service, we had stuffed it full of easily accessible distractions.[5] In the two decades that followed we searched diligently for ways to live as faithful stewards of media and technology. Our experiments throughout the years yielded both successes and failures. Our experiences and those of our students, families, and friends are retold in the pages that follow.

What does it mean to mindfully consume and critique media and technology in the light and Lordship of Jesus Christ?

With all that said, if you are looking for a book bashing media as excessively violent and gratuitously erotic,[6] it is not this one. If you are looking for one that recommends isolation from social media as the best solution for faithful Christian living, then you will be disappointed. Instead, in the chapters that follow we invite you to examine *mindfully* and ask new kinds of questions regarding your encounters as consumers, critics, and creators of all things media and technology in the light and Lordship of Jesus Christ. No easy task, but one that is worthwhile for all believers to undertake seriously.

THE BENEDICT OPTION

"The time was coming, said [Alasdair] MacIntyre, when men and women of virtue would understand that continued full participation in mainstream society was not possible for those who wanted to live a life of traditional virtue. These people would find new ways to live in community, he said, just as Saint Benedict, the sixth-century father of Western monasticism, responded to the collapse of Roman civilization by founding a monastic order. . . . The Benedict Option . . . idea [is] that serious Christian[s] . . . could no longer live business-as-usual lives in America, that we have to develop creative, communal solutions to help us hold on to our faith and our values in a world growing ever more hostile to them. We would have to choose to make a decisive leap into a truly countercultural way of living Christianity, or we would doom our children and our children's children to assimilation."[7]

—Rod Dreher, *The Benedict Option: A Strategy for Christians in a Post-Christian Nation*

In this introductory chapter, we present several key definitions and concepts, including popular, or "pop," culture, Sabbath, and mindfulness, to help you map a course for the conversations ahead. We conclude by explaining how cultivating what we call the *Three Sacreds*—sacred intentionality, sacred interiority, and sacred identity—can move you closer to faithful media stewardship and mindful (vs. mindless) engagement that distracts from your life's curriculum. Let's dance!

Dancing with Pop Culture

As critical consumers we recognize that pop culture has become the *locus theologicus* of our age, or the place where we live, where we "do" theology, and where we often encounter God.[8] Priestly and prophetic voices of the redemptive kind appear in some of the most unchurchy places, from *The Simpsons* to *The Lord of the Rings* to *LOST*.[9] And for better or worse we learn about the end-times from the *Left Behind* book series,[10] the creation story from the Creation Museum in Kentucky,[11] and the gruesome details of Christ's crucifixion from Mel Gibson's *The Passion of the Christ.*[12]

POP CULTURE AND WORLDVIEW

"I approach the popular arts, then, as part of the historical cultivation of God's creation carried on from generation to generation. The popular arts are not outside God's judgment—or beyond God's redemption. The challenge is to discover what it means for us to be faithful to God and responsible to our neighbor through these media."[13]

—William D. Romanowski, *Eyes Wide Open: Looking for God in Popular Culture*

Moreover, technological trends demonstrate that 70 percent of practicing Christian Millennials (ages 18–29) read Scripture on a screen, 54 percent are heavy users of online videos pertaining to faith or spirituality, and 59 percent search for spiritual content online.[14] How such digital immersion influences spiritual formation has yet to be fully determined.

Our Definition

We use *pop culture* as the umbrella term referring to all products (both media and technology) and activities within the mainstream of a given culture that are currently aimed at, and consumed by, the general public.[15] Pop culture includes three basic categories:

> We use *pop culture* as the umbrella term referring to all products (both media and technology) and activities within the mainstream of a given culture that are currently aimed at, and consumed by, the general public.

1. *Communication technologies* like smart phones, satellites, microchips, and apps that carry and distribute media content;

2. *Media content* like a film, a song, a book, an advertisement, a meme, or a television show, and how such content is used by and affects individuals, groups, and society; and

3. *Processes* and *practices* of various industries like Hollywood or Silicon Valley or Madison Avenue, and governmental organizations like the Federal Communications Commission (FCC) that surround and regulate communication technologies and determine how and when content is delivered.

Technology	Media	Processes
TV	Books	FCC
Apps	Music	Hollywood
Radio	Movies	Silicon Valley
Computer	TV Programs	Music Industry
Cell Phone	Advertisements	Madison Avenue

The term *media* also refers to both mass and social media. In *mass media* our interaction is generally one way. There is little or no interaction between artifact and audience. In contrast, *social media* are generally reciprocating. There is interaction between people who, to some degree, know each other. Social media may allow users to celebrate human relations mutually by sharing and being known.

Our Dance

We use the metaphor of pop culture as an unrelenting, always available dance partner. Said differently, *we cannot not dance with pop culture*. Well, we guess it is theoretically possible not to dance if you cut yourself off from media and technology like the sixteenth-century Luddites or twenty-first-century Amish. That means no smart phones, social media, movies, Super Bowl parties, or online shopping. You may not watch as much television or spend half your day on social media, but dancing is inevitable and daily for nearly everyone.

We cannot not dance with pop culture.

Understanding pop culture as a dance also requires us to extend our focus beyond immoral media content to include legitimate concerns about the various technologies and processes of communication themselves. Media and communication technologies are great gifts from God—products of his grace to be faithfully stewarded and used to bring about *shalom*, or the presence of God in our everyday relationships. We joyfully celebrate all benefits the tools of communication afford us as part of God's wondrous gifts of creation, from information to education to delight.

A GIFT OF GOD

Modern technology is "a gift of God which involves a great responsibility. . . . It is not technology which determines whether or not communication is authentic, but rather the human heart and our capacity to use wisely the means at our disposal."[16]

—Pope Francis, Fiftieth World Communications Day, January 24, 2016

At the same time, because these tools are formed from the earth's resources and human design, they suffer the effects of humanity's fall into sin. Along with all creation, they groan from the pain of sin and wait eagerly to be liberated from their bondage of decay (Rom. 8:19–21).

We are not suggesting that technology itself is a sin or even determinative. As the quote from Pope Francis above indicates, people still act or fail to act based on free will and their interpretation of certain messages. What we are suggesting is that *technology is not neutral*. When it comes to technology it is well known that "We shape our tools, and thereafter our tools shape us."[17] Each technology has its own unique DNA or characteristic predispositions that affect how messages are constructed and delivered, and it shapes the mind, body, and spirit of individuals immersed in their use.[18] There are no super-human, extra-special-person exceptions here—everyone is affected to some degree.

We are wise to avoid technological idolatry and develop technological literacy.

For instance, while your smart phone does not make you do anything immoral, it certainly does influence the way you interact with others, and it can easily distract you during times of quiet prayer and devotion. Playing video games is fun but it may desensitize you to violence. Television delivers important news and rich entertainment but encourages you to think that seeing is believing. The Internet is a superhighway of helpful information, but over time it may chip away at your capacity to concentrate and meditate for extended periods of time. Social media connects you with friends and family but may actually lower your ability to empathize with others.[19] As such, we are wise to develop *technological literacy* and avoid *technological idolatry*, or the belief that there is an app for every personal or social problem we encounter and that all we need is the latest gadget to set us on the proper social, intellectual, and spiritual paths.

TECHNOLOGICAL LITERACY

1. "What values are inherent in this medium (my TV, PC, and cell phone)?"

2. "What impact does this medium have on my relationship with others and with God?"

3. "What impact do various social institutions such as the family, business, or government have on why and how we use certain technologies?"[20]

—Bill Strom, *More Than Talk: Communication Studies and the Christian Faith*

More importantly, if the kind of inevitability we describe above is even partially true, then our dance with pop culture helps frame the crucible of our existence and posits a question of moral and spiritual significance: *Who is leading whom in the dance*? Are we dancing in the dark, comfortably unaware or in blatant denial of our pop culture rituals and patterns of self-justifying behavior that keep us from more faithful Sabbath living? Or are we dancing in the light, mindfully guided in our pop culture choices by the overarching responsibility of living redemptively, moment by moment, acknowledging the responsibility of wisdom, love, and good deeds?

> Who is leading whom in your pop culture dance?

In short, many of us live underexamined pop culture lives. We underestimate our time and energy spent in the dance and our partner's unprecedented ability to attract our attention nearly all the time. We bury deep a secret belief that its rhythms are functionally superior to other, face-to-face options before us. Put another way, what many people long for but find difficult to experience amidst the digital noise and distraction is Sabbath rest.

THE MAIN QUESTION

"The main question raised by pop culture concerns the most edifying way to spend one's time."[21]

—Kenneth A. Myers, *All God's Children and Blue Suede Shoes*

Sabbath Living as Cultural Resistance

If you lived in Puritan New England in the seventeenth century, then you most likely took the Sabbath as one day of rest seriously. Businesses and stores were closed on Sunday so people could attend church, and nearly everyone did. Up through the early twentieth century until the late 1960s such practices were still common across much of the United States, especially in the South. But today, in a post-Christian society consumed by consumption, busyness, and productivity, observing the Sabbath seems flat-out countercultural.

The Sabbath, or the Lord's Day, is the subject of God's fourth commandment to the Israelites in Deuteronomy 5:12. It instructs the people to find rest by refraining from work on the seventh day of the week, from sundown on Friday to sundown on Saturday. The day was a gift from God so Israel could remember him and how he brought them out of Egypt: how he *literally* and *figuratively* kept them from being imprisoned slaves. The Sabbath was a day focused on physical and mental rejuvenation. It intended to reorient radically humanity's view of work and rest and, thereby, keep them from another form of enslavement. For the Christian tradition, the Lord's Day was generally changed from Saturday to Sunday.

Have you ever thought about the Sabbath in these terms? How does it change your own Sabbath keeping?

Importantly, the author of the New Testament book of Hebrews makes no distinction between the legal demands of the seventh day and the experience of rest that Israel was to experience *every day* in the promised land. Thus, as God desired that Israel enter into his "Sabbath-rest" as they crossed into the promised land, so our Creator desires that our daily existence be characterized by a life of freeing, energizing rest (Heb. 4:1–13, NIV). Sabbath rest, then, is not just about a promised land-experience one day of the week by taking Sunday off to relax, but about an everyday experience that permeates the whole of life.

In this light, Sabbath is more than just following rules that express what you cannot do on a particular day of the week. Old Testament scholar Walter Brueggemann explains that Sabbath is best understood as a pattern of *resistance* to the dominant cultural insistence that human worth is reduced to

 Sabbath can be understood as a pattern of resistance to the dominant culture.

our productivity as labor units. It implies resistance to our never-ending culture of consumption that grounds human value and identity in achievement and possession. In essence, Sabbath prophetically challenges taken-for-granted assumptions of the cultural status quo about the quality and meaning of life.[22]

KEEPING THE SABBATH

"If you keep the Sabbath, you start to see creation not as somewhere to get away from your ordinary life, but a place to frame an attentiveness to your life."[23]

—Eugene H. Peterson, *The Pastor: A Memoir*

As it relates to pop culture, Sabbath constitutes our resistance to surrender to every entertainment impulse and technological option surrounding us. We become imprisoned by pop culture when, through our lack of *mindful* monitoring and moderating, consumption becomes excessive and mindless. In this sense, Sabbath is about becoming a whole person, not one easily fragmented by the 24/7 bombardment of pop cultural delights competing for our loyalties and passions. Deepening our experience with Sabbath graces helps us to break the restless consumptive cycle. It helps us avoid being imprisoned by the culture's tyranny of the now, the dictates of self-indulgence, and concentrate on what is really important: God. Neighbors. All of life. In so doing, we experience the rest God intended for his human creation every day.

How do you avoid becoming Sabbath deprived? Sabbath poor? Sabbath-less?

For instance, when our wondering about whether the Detroit Tigers will win tonight overshadows the daily arena in which we live and affect change, we are Sabbath-deprived. When the major dramatic question of the day is whether our favorite reality show contestant will get voted off, we are Sabbath-poor. When we interrupt face-to-face encounters to check our handheld devices obsessively for incoming messages, we are Sabbath-less. When our yearning for alternative vistas, landscapes, or planets trumps the sacred moments of our daily existence, we have lost touch with Sabbath richness and rest.

SABBATH AS FREEDOM

"[The Sabbath is] for freedom, a day on which we would not use the instruments which have been so easily turned into weapons of destruction, a day for being with ourselves, a day of detachment from the vulgar, . . . a day on which we stop worshipping the idols of technical civilization . . . ."[24]

—Abraham Joshua Heschel, *I Asked for Wonder*

How then do we experience Sabbath rest in our high tech, image-dominated, "amused-to-death" pop culture landscape? This book suggests at least two ways.

First, many sources talk about experiencing Sabbath *away* or *apart from* pop culture by strategically and regularly unplugging or detaching.[25] Your authors personally practice and encourage such activities as you will see in this book. When practiced regularly and with intentionality, such fasting can be illuminating and lead to the kind of everyday Sabbath we describe above. However, given the normal demands of life, most people we know find it terribly difficult to regularly practice fasting and tend to give up after a few attempts, believing that being tethered to their devices is the new normal.

Thus, we also propose and explore a second, less frequently discussed possibility, which is experiencing everyday Sabbath *in or with* pop culture through the practice of *mindful engagement* or *attachment*. This kind of engagement does not require us to wait for Sunday to roll around, unplug for a day, or go on a silent retreat to experience true Sabbath rest.

Mindfulness is active, open attention to the present moment. It can be developed through practice and training.

Mindfulness, or what we describe as *mindful attachment,* is a state of active, open attention to the present moment that can be developed through the deliberate practice and training of self-reflection and critical contemplation. When mindfully engaged, you bring your full attention to the internal and external experiences occurring in the present moment as you simultaneously contextualize them within the larger meta-narrative, or story to which you belong.

SACRED MOMENTS

"There is something sacred in every moment."[26]

—Abraham Joshua Heschel, *God in Search of Man: A Philosophy of Judaism*

The goal of mindfulness from a *Christian* perspective is to refocus away from the clutter of your life to the gift of the moment, or the gift of the presence of the grace that engulfs us; to encounter reality through God's eyes, with his ears, and all of his senses as part of a faithful and connected community. This human-divine perspective-taking makes us more ourselves, or more who God intended us to be while helping us avoid the kind of self-indulgence or hyper-individualism that often accompanies our consumption.

SACRED ATTACHMENT

"There is need for detachment—a 'sabbath of contemplation' as Peter of Celles, a Benedictine monk of the twelfth century, put it. But there is a danger in thinking only in terms of detachment as Jesus indicates in his story of the man who had been emptied of evil but not filled with good . . .; we must go on to attachment. The detachment from the confusion all around us is in order to have a richer attachment to God."[27]

—Richard J. Foster, *Celebration of Discipline: The Path to Spiritual Growth*

To help promote mindful engagement with pop culture, we explore three key constructs in this book:

1. *Sacred Intentionality* (chapters 3–4), or intentionality toward the sacred in our pop culture engagement that helps us connect each pop culture moment to life's overarching purposes, including our loving service of God and neighbor;

2. *Sacred Interiority* (chapters 5–6), or the development of an interior life and mind focused on the sacred that helps us to draw on relevant biblical truths under the Holy Spirit's promptings in response to the anticipated and unanticipated effects of pop culture; and

3. *Sacred Identity* (chapters 7–8), or a sense of self firmly rooted in a biblical understanding of personhood that emphasizes the development of an internal locus of self-identity to help combat the external sense of self that dominates social media and celebrity culture.

Throughout, we suggest that cultivating these *Three Sacreds* help us to avoid "dancing in a trance" (chapter 2) and develop instead a biblically informed mindfulness with our pop culture dance partner.

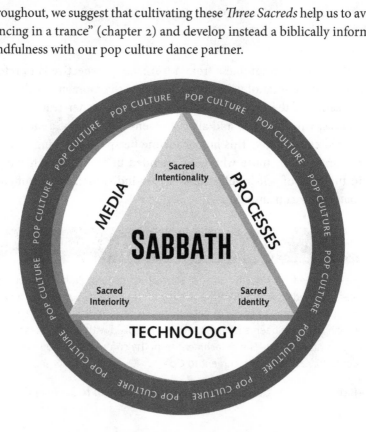

Sixteenth-century theologian and spiritual leader St. Ignatius of Loyola describes a "holy habit" as any intentional action done repeatedly over time with the goal of being formed into Christ-likeness and growing in love for God and others. Like other "holy habits" such as prayer or meditation, mindful pop culture engagement fueled by the *Three Sacreds* can deepen one's faith and promote faithfulness, wisdom, and virtue in our communication with God, self, and others.[28] Regularly practicing mindful engagement in relation to pop culture cultivates the heart-and-mind habit of alertness to the presence, power, and provision of God in every moment. It helps us mentally submit our entertainment desires to God's reality. This

"Holy habits" cultivate Christlikeness and help us grow in our love for God and neighbor.

Sabbath-oriented holy habit ultimately allows us to avoid treating pop culture as an end in and of itself and to avoid disjointed or divided affections that drain energy, purpose, and identity.

PROMOTING EVERYDAY SABBATH

1. What is the purpose of my existence in God's created order, and how does a particular pop culture artifact mirror that purpose?

2. What does it mean to be a human being created in God's image, and how is humanness represented in the pop culture artifact?

3. What is the nature of reality and truth in God's created order, and in what ways does the pop culture artifact I am consuming reflect that reality and truth?

Conclusion

We do not suspect most people on their deathbeds wish they played one more video game, saw one more cheesy ad for body deodorant, or watched one more episode of their favorite program. As embarrassing as our Sunday afternoon football fiasco is to admit, we are grateful for the wake-up call.

Sabbath as a daily habit not only promotes rest and rejuvenation but also protects us from death of purpose, identity, and kingdom service. Sabbath is the life-giving, life-affirming grace-response that provides context to all of life's choices and breathes life into our roles as pop culture critics, creators, and consumers. Sabbath works as an everyday pattern of resistance that disentangles us from the dominance of spectator passivity. And when faithfully cultivated, the *Three Sacreds*—sacred intentionality, sacred interiority, and sacred

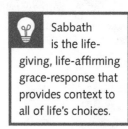

Sabbath is the life-giving, life-affirming grace-response that provides context to all of life's choices.

identity—can help us move from being *mindless* spectators to *mindful* Sabbath dwellers with pop culture.

In our next chapter we suggest that the key to understanding when we are engaging mindfully with pop culture begins with the challenging work of self-examination. Our habits of comfort and rest, and especially our distraction patterns, are portions of the dance rarely explored. Without such self-analysis, we may end up in a pop culture trance dance that robs us of everyday Sabbath.

Let's Get Practical

1. Introduce yourself to the habit of monitoring by starting a pop culture journal and writing in it for several minutes each day. Start with five minutes and work your way up to fifteen minutes a day. To begin, for one week, monitor your engagement and keep track of the conditions of your use, especially focused on the amount of time you are spending with different pop culture. What did you learn about your habits and patterns? For example, what is the first thing you reach for in the morning? What prompts certain kinds of use? What media or technology could you not see yourself living without?

2. Consider starting a list of your "Top 5" daily encounters with pop culture such as movies, novels, concerts, televised sports events, and so forth. Have a conversation with a friend and compare lists. What did you learn? What changes will you make in your daily encounters with pop culture? Include your reflections in your pop culture journal.

3. Go on a one-mile walk for ten straight days. The walks are not about exercise. No devices, no headphones allowed. Be tech free. During your walks, become familiar with your "stream-of-consciousness" (i.e., what you find yourself thinking about without the distractions of media or technology). What comes to mind when you are not filling it with pop culture? As with everything in the "Let's Get Practical" section at the end of each chapter, enter your reflections into your pop culture journal.

Discussion Questions

1. Someone who read about your authors' football fiasco in the opening paragraphs of this chapter said, "Sounds like time well spent to me, and I know others who would agree." How might you respond?

2. In what ways do social media produce the kind of "spectator passivity" described by your authors in the opening paragraphs?

3. What does the Sabbath mean to you? Is keeping the Sabbath or experiencing everyday Sabbath difficult for you?

4. Of the *Three Sacreds*, which one do you think presents the greatest challenge to you when it comes to experiencing everyday Sabbath?

Chapter 2

Dancing in a Trance
(Amusing Ourselves to Death)

"Americans no longer talk to each other, they entertain [and amuse] each other [to death]. They do not exchange ideas; they exchange images. They do not argue with propositions; they argue with good looks, celebrities and commercials."[1]

—NEIL POSTMAN,
COMMUNICATION THEORIST AND CULTURAL CRITIC

"Although they claimed to be wise, they became fools and exchanged the glory of the immortal God for images made to look like a mortal human being and birds and animals and reptiles. Therefore God gave them over in the sinful desires of their hearts to sexual impurity for the degrading of their bodies with one another."

—ROMANS 1:22-24 (NIV)

DANCE MARATHONS BECAME A distracting phenomenon in the 1920s and 1930s, a compelling sideshow to the harsh realities of the Great Depression. Hundreds, sometimes thousands, of couples converged on massive dance floors and danced until they literally dropped. These were dance endurance contests. The last man and woman standing won.

At first, the dancing was energized and precise. But hours of elegant and purposeful movement eventually gave way to zombie-like trance dancing as stiff-limbed couples swayed slowly to the music with vacant stares. To the casual observer dancers appeared to be sleepwalking, much like today's "smartphone zombies" who walk slowly with head tilts and without attention to their surroundings.

In this chapter, we suggest that many of our patterns of pop culture interaction turn a segment of us, however inadvertently, into unknowing participants in a dance marathon. We call this our *mediated trance dance*. This implies that we occasionally sleepwalk with pop culture, in part, due to a business-as-usual approach to our discretionary time and a lack of mindfulness. Of course, we never see ourselves as being in a trance dance; that is one standard characteristic of a trance.[2]

To avoid the trance dance, we invite readers to do the tough work of self-reflection that leads to greater awareness of the regular rhythms of work and rest. We begin by introducing several cycles of engagement toward pop culture that most of us exhibit and that, if left unchecked, can lull us into believing that our current routine is the new digital normal. Over time these cycles can contribute to our embrace of certain "default modes" of consumption, including reward-viewing, relief-viewing, and resignation-viewing, which further alienate us from mindful living and redemptive use of

> To avoid the trance dance we must reflect on our life's rhythms and identify default modes of pop culture consumption.

our time. We conclude by suggesting that understanding the dual nature of boredom as both a catalyst of creativity and a distractor of purpose can help a person redeem the mundane moments of life and participate more mindfully with pop culture.

Cycles of Engagement

In one of our classes, students keep a pop culture journal for one week so they can understand how their life's rhythms are influenced by media and technology. One student wrote the following:

> My alarm app wakes me around 7 am with happy music. I slowly roll over, hit snooze, grab my phone and with eyes half shut check the news alerts that arrived during the night. I click on my social media feed, then text messages, then email, and then voice mail

"just in case" (I mean, who leaves voice mail anymore?!?!?!). Just about that time the alarm goes off again and I drag myself from bed and stumble like a drunkin' mummy to the bathroom by the light of my phone, some mornings tripping over the dog. I check my phone a few more times, then put in my earbuds to drown out the people around me as I head to the kitchen. During breakfast I read my devotional Bible app but find it difficult to stay focused most days due to interrupting messages from friends. On my way to work I'll order coffee using my Starbuck's app, listen to my playlist, download my favorite program to watch later, and call one of my best friends to decide where we are going to eat dinner. When I get to work I video chat with my parents in the parking lot before I start work.

 ## FORMING HABITS

University College, London, conducted a study with 96 people and found that it takes on average 66 days to create, form, or break a habit. They found that it was easier to start a new habit than break a bad one, but it takes about the same amount of time. The best way to break a habit, according to researchers, is to start a new habit.[3]

Her afternoon and evening entries included much of the same, the day bracketed by newsfeeds and email and messaging with friends during and after classes. Each day she reported spending more time on average communicating with her friends and co-workers through digital messaging than in person; she turned to her social media feed mainly to help reduce stress and pass the time when she was bored. Five of the seven days she spent at least two hours before bed catching up with episodes of her latest favorite program. Then, "lights out" (on her screen, at least) around midnight, just after she said her prayers that she read from her favorite devotional app.

The activities listed in her journal seemed comparable to taking a stimulant drug of some kind the minute we woke up or drinking five cups

> Cycles of engagement toward pop culture can become habits of the heart that lead us into a mediated trance dance if not carefully monitored and moderated.

of coffee, totally wired, before rolling out of bed. As our student's not-so-uncommon entry illustrates, many of us are doing the digital equivalent of that every morning.

For better or worse and in sickness and in health, we each have our own daily rhythm with pop culture that we slip in and out of without much warning—or, quite frankly, without much thinking. These rhythms bring order to our day and set our priorities. Yet our constant and often mindless consumption of new information from dawn's early light can lead to decision fatigue, lack of focus, or worry before our day ever really gets going. The tiny hits of dopamine our brains receive from messaging leave us either dependent on that for the rest of the day or deflated because we are not getting any more.

ADDICTED TO INFORMATION

Do you ever find it nearly impossible to ignore your incoming messages when you hear that sound? According to researchers, much of what we do online releases dopamine into the brain's pleasure centers the same way as cocaine and other stimulant drugs, which makes you feel enjoyment, pleasure, and motivates you to seek out certain behaviors such as food, sex, drugs, and yes, information. Over time we get drawn into a dopamine-induced loop. Dopamine starts us seeking, and the rewards we get for the seeking drive our compulsion to continually check email, news, and social media in anticipation of receiving good news.[4]

Over time, reading student journal entries along with our own experiences led us to identify at least five *cycles of engagement*, or regularly repeated behaviors, attitudes, and assumptions toward pop culture that can contribute to a mediated trance dance.

We Underexamine

In a media environment flooded with distractions and time fillers, our choices about how to make use of our time provide us with clues to the purposes of our hearts.[5] Yet rarely does our self-examination focus on being thoughtful of the motivations, habits, benefits, and burdens of our pop culture engagement. For most of our students, the journal assignment is the first time they have ever done any serious pop culture soul-searching. Certainly, it is important to be aware of the marketing techniques that draw us in for the next 120 minutes to another four episodes of our favorite program. But *equally* important to know is what makes us *willing*, or perhaps *needing*, to invest 120 minutes of our lives catching up on last year's episodes of that program.

 NOTICING SELF

"And men go abroad to wonder at the heights of mountains, the huge waves of the sea, the broad streams of rivers, the vastness of the ocean, and the turnings of the stars—and they do not notice themselves."[6]

—Saint Augustine of Hippo, fifth century Church Father

Admonitions similar to Plato's oft quoted "know thyself"[7] appear centuries earlier in the Bible. In Psalm 139:23–24 the psalmist David invites the Lord to "search me" to "know my heart" and my "anxious thoughts" (NIV). God already knew David's heart, but David's invitation triggered a daily process of self-discovery. The book of Proverbs echoes "know thyself" but describes it as "giving thought to one's ways." In Proverbs 20:5 the wise person is encouraged to know the "purposes of his heart" since the purposes driving our actions and attitudes are sometimes "deep waters" that require heavy spiritual lifting to "draw them out" (NIV). This kind of self-awareness is an essential part of the process that leads to greater spiritual growth, including knowledge of the purposes and patterns behind our pop culture engagement.

Sometimes our self-examination about pop culture habits falls short because we wrongly assume that bad habits come mainly from consuming certain kinds of illicit or morally questionable R-rated content, as if all we need to consume is positive, family-friendly fare and virtuous habits will follow. Although habitually watching large chunks of Christian or other family-friendly programming might allow us to congratulate ourselves for avoiding entertainment "trash," it also enables us to miss the more important point of the sacredness of our purpose-filled existence and, therefore, the redemptive use of time. The habit of self-examination in

> What makes you willing to invest so much time from your life in pop culture?

our pop culture-saturated setting requires monitoring and moderating our "entertain me" sensibility, even if our viewing appetites are dominated by family-friendly classics.

THE SELF-EXAMINATION APP

Heartpoints, an app developed by Yed Anikpo and Christian Apps LLC, is "a GPS for the Christian heart." Users "check in" their activities of the day and then review their history to repent or give thanks. Good "check-ins" can be shared with friends and family. Anikpo hopes Heartpoints helps Christians commune "with our hearts in silence" rather than stay "busy amusing ourselves to death with our gadget." Ultimately, the goal is to help Christians "restore" the "lost Christian virtues of watching and self-examination."[8] While supporters praise the app's "check-in to my heart" notifications and user-friendly interface, critics are concerned that "this app is exactly what Christianity shouldn't be: an over-simplified, legalistic checklist." They further wonder whether using the app encourages us to rely "upon ourselves to monitor and increase our holiness" rather than on the Holy Spirit "living within us, actively reshaping our desires and making us more like Jesus."[9] Do you side with the supporters or critics? Would you use this app?

We Give Undivided Attention

Our always available and varied pop culture options are a veritable feast for unsatisfied eyes. The entertainment spectacles winning our attention have a unique ability to attract a repeated trance-like focus through eye-catching technical changes and effective storytelling.

Next time you are at a restaurant with monitors on the walls, sit directly in front of one so you can see how often the programming interferes with your own and others' conversations. Even with the sound muted the flashing technical changes—i.e., camera angle, focus, or any camera movement—draw eyes to the screen like moths to a flame. Imagine being in conversation with the prophet Jeremiah in one of these places. In mid-sentence we excuse ourselves to watch a pinch-hit home run or celebrity highlight over the prophet's left shoulder, and then text a friend about it. We would probably do the same if we were talking with Jesus.

In hardly any other time in history can our capacity to focus, which is a great gift of God, be so intensely employed and exhausted. As twentieth-century Methodist missionary E. Stanley Jones quipped, "What gets your attention, gets you."[10] And pop culture is increasingly brilliant at grabbing us and demanding intensely singular focus. So brilliant, in fact, that one dad, fed up with his son's inability to break free from playing video games with friends, created an app called ReplyASAP that allows parents to send a message to their kids' phones that freezes their devices until they respond to their parents.[11]

YOUR BRAIN ON SNAPCHAT

Jane Raymond, award-winning professor of visual cognition at the University of Birmingham, consults with companies on how best to deliver brand messaging in ads. According to Raymond, our brains "gulp" messaging and imagery. Our brains consume the first bit but then need several seconds to digest it before consuming the next amount. In that small moment of waiting for the next bit or byte of data, our undivided, gulping brain hones in on our phone with laser-like focus. Some social media have begun to capitalize on this tendency, especially Snapchat. Alarms could be sounding off all around, but with Snapchat you only have six seconds to view the message before it is gone forever![12]

We do not suggest that all pop culture is trance-like. Certainly, part of pop culture's intense draw is its ability to involve us at a variety of attention levels. And many things in life outside pop culture grab our undivided attention at trance-like levels as well. The point is that mediated pop culture options will, in most instances, more readily trigger our capacity for intense, singular focus.

Pop culture's ability to nurture our singular focus is also inherent in the power of a story well told. A large percentage of media content is narrative. Whether it is the bottom of the ninth with the home team down one run, or the frenzy of a second-act chase scene in an action-adventure movie, we are suckers for good stories. In fact, we are wired to be drawn to the power of stories. We are *homo narrans*, or storytelling persons, created in the image and likeness of a storytelling God who knows that stories help keep the attention of our easily distracted selves.[13]

YOUR BRAIN ON STORIES

University of California, Berkeley, researchers discovered that storytelling engages your brain more than math or music. Listening to stories triggers memories and emotions on the left and right sides of the brain. Engaging a story requires social and spatial reasoning and visual imagery. Scientists may one day be able to "read" the brains of people who cannot speak due to stroke or disease.[14]

We are also drawn to stories because we are uniquely created to extend empathy to any protagonist with a difficult set of obstacles keeping him or her from a desired goal. Without fail, well-told stories strengthen our empathetic capacity as we are giving opportunity to provisionally practice "walking in someone else's shoes." The result, ideally, is that we are more fully capable of the loving acts of service toward others who are struggling with obstacles. As Abraham Joshua Heschel rightly observed, "Empathy rather than expression is the way of piety."[15]

King David—who was once caught up in a powerful story's trap told by the prophet Nathan (2 Sam. 12:1–7)—prayed that the Lord would give him an "undivided heart" in order to fear God's name. King David's use of the term "heart" in this case was referring to the source of his ultimate passions, his life's energies and direction (Ps. 86:11b, NIV). He wanted everything he loved and desired—friendships, wisdom, entertainment, and intimacy—to be ordered only in relation to his ultimate love for God and an undivided attention to the divine story.

We Consider It Superior

A friend recently called us in a panic after his adult son stopped going out, taking calls, or maintaining relationships with family and friends. All he wanted to do was watch movies and play video games in his man cave. Apparently, the movies helped him to transcend his self-described daily tedium. The gaming offered convenient progress reports and tangible rewards for even the smallest success. If only the rest of life were that exciting.

> Why do many of our pop culture encounters seem superior to almost any other kinds of experiences?

Even if we do not fit this extreme example, we all share something in common with our friend's son. Too often our pop culture choices are deemed superior in outcome and excitement to anything three-dimensionally available to us: any friend, any ministry opportunity, any thought, anything, period. Rather than strike up a conversation with a stranger on a plane or in line at the grocery store, or have a conversation with God through prayer, we pull out our devices to avoid any awkward pauses or viewpoints that challenge our taken-for-granted assumptions.

Let's be honest, mediated encounters require far less effort and are much easier to disengage from when we are not satisfied. If they do not deliver—for example, because we do not win the argument or draw positive praise for our "insightful" point of view—we change the channel, revise our status, or block a "friend." Given this kind of increased control, positive outcomes and successes are almost always guaranteed. Pop culture becomes the always-on-call trump card to help a person exist with the possibility of life-moments that are less than interesting and with people who are less than exhilarating.

EVERY DECISION MATTERS

"Every decision a person makes . . . will take him toward or away from a relationship with the Person who made him, the one relationship for which that person was created."[16]

—Armand Nicholi, Clinical Professor of Psychology, Harvard Medical School

Indeed, friends or family regularly join us in shared mediated experiences. Shared, yes, but rarely do they involve post-event conversations where truths are separated from half-truths or reality distinguished from manufactured images. Unlike three-dimensional experiences, two-dimensional ones do not let us view them with others from different angles. There is only a surface, but the surface is often more seductive than the reality and the hard work that come with some (self-) depth perception.

When the choice before us is between loving service and personal pleasure, the latter usually wins. The mind and heart have the habit of wanting to repeat what they find pleasurable. Like our friend's son, we regularly and secretly believe that real life simply cannot compete with the escape found in the gratification of reaching the next level of a video game.[17]

We Underestimate

On the first day of our pop culture class each semester, before we dismiss students, we regularly share research that reports how mobile users check their phones up to 150 times a day; send, receive, or avoid twenty-two phone calls every day and send or receive messages twenty-three times a day; and that most people cannot go six minutes without checking their phone.[18] We then ask students to estimate the number of times they check their mobile devices each day. Answers range from ten to twenty-five times a day. Finally, we ask them to compare their estimates with their actual phone usage logs for the last two days and raise their hands if their

Why do we tend to underestimate our time spent with pop culture?

estimates were wrong. In less than five minutes all hands are raised. Stunned silence. Without exception, students underestimate by two to three times their actual amount of use.

The process usually goes something like this: we begin by first underestimating the time spent trying to figure out *what* to consume. Then once we settle in for a minute or an hour, we cannot help underestimating that time either. In the meantime, our inner monologue struggles to justify the unfocused free falling with discretionary time through the wilderness of freedom and unlimited choices. And on it goes.

PARENTS DON'T UNDERSTAND

According to research, parents severely underestimate the time their children spend on digital devices. Approximately 83 percent of children between the ages of 10 and 17 estimate they use an electronic device for three or more hours each day. However, a separate survey of parents revealed that only 40 percent of parents believe their children use an electronic device for that same amount of time.[19]

For many, spending time with pop culture is like going to a grocery store without a shopping list. Without a list to guide our shopping, we stroll (or "scroll for the sake of scrolling") mindlessly through the aisles of choices, all the while forgetting a short list in our back pocket of the nourishment that is missing from our pantry. The decision to select certain items is a response to a variety of things other than our list, including superficial attention grabbers like the food's placement on the shelf or its flashy packaging. Our choices are too frequently driven by our impulses toward a craving or secret addiction. If we are not aware of the time we are spending, it inevitably consumes far more of our time and budget than we realize.[20] And if the local grocery store was as accessible as our devices and entertainment choices, ready to meet our every food whim, we would probably spend more time there than in school, church, or with loved ones, and our physical health would suffer.[21]

We Embrace "Default Modes"

As teachers we would come home after evening classes with our minds racing. Although tired, we were not ready for bed. If the class went well (or did not), we would treat ourselves to our favorite food. We deserved it, after all, no matter what our spouses or doctors said. This was our self-congratulatory eating ritual.

HUMAN DEFAULT MODES

"A fundamental insight of Martin Luther's was that 'religion' is the default mode of the human heart. Your computer operates automatically in a default mode unless you deliberately tell it to do something else. So Luther says that even after you are converted by the gospel your heart will go back to operating on other principles unless you deliberately, repeatedly set it to gospel-mode. We habitually and instinctively look to other things besides God and his grace as our justification, hope, significance, and security."[22]

—Timothy Keller, *The Prodigal God: Recovering the Heart of the Christian Faith*

This act of ritual indulgence was a habit we formed over many years. Like most habits and some rituals, it was done unthinkingly. It became our default mode in a variety of circumstances.[23] We have identified three types of pop culture ritual indulgence that are just as self-congratulatory and unhealthy as our post-class eating ritual.

1. **"I've Earned This Dance": Reward-Viewing.** Like your authors' post-class eating ritual, pop culture consumption is regularly experienced as a reward, or entitlement, for work successfully (or unsuccessfully) completed. This is rooted in the positive work-and-Sabbath-rest cycle that is God's wise plan for healthy human functioning. After all, we *should* seek opportunities for refreshment after time spent working, right?

But this kind of default viewing contributes to self-indulgence and a lack of discipline. Part of the problem is that in our legitimate seeking of Sabbath rest as an everyday experience, we lean too heavily on pop culture's availability. There is a sense of entitlement that lurks behind our self-permission to wander the cyber dance floor, sometimes embracing lurid partners. It also provides an excuse for consuming entertainment alone at home or messaging with distant others while physically surrounded by family. With multiple screens in nearly every room, it is pretty easy

> Our habits toward pop culture take years to form. They represent our heart's desires.

to watch alone—an extension of what sociologists call the "bowling alone" phenomenon.[24]

2. "I Need This Dance": Relief-Viewing. Art, whether in the form of Leonardo da Vinci's *Mona Lisa* or a gripping television drama, invites us to take a break from the demands of our life. And it is important for us to experience this kind of comfort. Internally, we seek relief from worries and emotional pains. Externally, we seek relief from deafening silence as well as loud, threatening voices. Pop culture is often used to provide a sedative kind of relief from our uncertainties and fears.

It may help to imagine relief-viewing along a continuum of psychic survival. On the one end of the continuum the internal voice asks, "How am I going to survive the tedium of the next hour?" On the other end of the continuum is a serious existentialist crisis that screams, "How am I going to get through the agony of a meaningless life?"

THE BEGINNER'S MIND

"Beginner's mind is a posture of eagerness, of spiritual hunger. The beginner's mind knows it needs something. This is a rare feeling in today's treacherously seductive culture, however. Because it [culture] is so immediately satisfying, it is hard to remain spiritually hungry. We give answers too quickly, take away pain too easily, and too quickly stimulate."[25]

—Richard Rohr, *Everything Belongs: The Gift of Contemplative Prayer*

As with reward-viewing, though, problems arise when relief-viewing is our go-to response in moments of stress or tedium. Sedatives work well on occasion, but to maintain their positive effects over time you must gradually increase the dosage.

3. "There's Nothing Else to Do But Dance": Resignation-Viewing. In addition to reward- and relief-viewing, we regularly turn to pop culture because we tell ourselves, "There's nothing else to do," or we are bored. Over time, such resignation-viewing can push family, friends, and ministry to the margins of life. So, what do you *do* when you do not *have to do* anything?

For Søren Kierkegaard, the nineteenth-century Danish theologian and philosopher, boredom is evidence of a spiritual disorder. It is the gateway to existential crisis and possibly "evil" (see Prov. 16:27, NIV). Being bored

UNBORABLE?

"To be, in a word, unborable. . . . It is the key to modern life. If you are immune to boredom, there is literally nothing you cannot accomplish."[26]

—David Foster Wallace, *The Pale King*

is symptomatic of a person ruled by a view of reality that excludes the presence of God. To Kierkegaard, boredom is the "dark side of a life devoted to amusement and pleasure."[27] He persistently provoked his audience about their game plans once the amusement ceased to amuse.[28]

Although we recognize the reality of boredom's dark side, it is important to highlight the dual nature of boredom and the importance of remaining "pro-boredom." As people created for Sabbath rest, we are wired to seek temporary landscapes to replace the depressed, uninteresting, or broken ones. This is not a bad thing. In fact, this is the Sabbath-related function of most art and entertainment: to give us a provisional experience that relaxes us when our pace becomes exhausting and rejuvenates us when our assumptions become stale.

Plus, many of our important ideas and learning moments come in the shower or gardening, as we perform mundane activities, as our brain

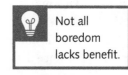

Not all boredom lacks benefit.

wanders and we experience eureka moments of creativity, passion, and inspiration. So, filling every one of those moments—whether in the shower or garden, or at an airport or waiting on a bus or at doctor's office—with information or entertainment gathering, no matter how uplifting, would rob us of that quiet processing time. Granted, this is an increasingly difficult

PRO-BOREDOM

As researcher Andreas Elpidorou of the University of Louisville explains, "Boredom helps to restore the perception that one's activities are meaningful or significant," meaning that it acts as a "regulatory state that keeps one in line with one's projects. In the absence of boredom, one would remain trapped in unfulfilling situations, and miss out on many emotionally, cognitively, and socially rewarding experiences. Boredom is both a warning that we are not doing what we want to be doing and a 'push' that motivates us to switch goals and projects."[29]

> "Redemptive boredom" is bounded boredom, or boredom guided by purpose.

challenge since, compared to Kierkegaard's nineteenth-century Europe, today's amusements are so varied and readily available that the habits of the mind can function as if the dance will never end. With television (the "first screen"), and the avalanche of Internet invitations (the "second screen"), there is always the certainty that something is next.

"Redemptive boredom" occurs when it is *bounded* boredom, or boredom with a *telos*, or ultimate purpose. Put another way, when our default mode in response to life's listless moments is to seek pop culture's messianic intervention, and we give in to "our inability to faithfully regard the holiness of things,"[30] boredom's dark side triumphs. In such instances, mediated electronic frames fly us to exotic settings and dramatic heights while ensuring us that each two-dimensional option is superior to the dullness of the three-dimensional moment literally staring us in the face. It is only later— or never—that we come to realize the wasted time and folly of our ways.

As with reward- and relief-viewing, resignation-viewing is a type of ritual viewing. If the rationale for viewing is repeated and the entertainment-seeking pursuit is satisfied, then the activity becomes part of a daily rhythm that provides order to our lives and contributes to our mediated trance dance.

AVOIDING THE TRANCE DANCE

1. Is my engagement in mass media or social media about reward-, relief-, or resignation-viewing?

2. Is there any emotional agitation provoking the intervention of mass media or social media engagement? If so, what specifically is the nature of the agitation? Is it boredom, or is it irritation or frustration?

3. Is engagement in mass media or social media negatively affecting potential face-to-face conversations?

Conclusion

Apart from the occasional charity event, dance marathons are a thing of the past. Nonetheless, they serve as helpful reminders of our tendency to dance in a trance with pop culture.

A key to understanding our dance with pop culture is doing the hard work that leads to greater self-awareness and alertness. Alert to our learned default modes. Alert to our habits of work and rest. And, especially, alert to the triggers that lead to distraction. These are important issues since they provide significant hints to the longings and loves that mark us.

Monitoring our pop culture pursuits can lead to transformational awareness and new holy habits.

It is a God-ordained impulse to seek rest and comforts in Sabbath-like activities, including pop culture. However, if left unmonitored our tech pursuits and entertainment seeking can subtly become a disproportionate focus of our existence.

In our next six chapters (3–8) we discuss how to cultivate healthy patterns and habits of pop culture to confront our increased vulnerability to trance dancing. We begin with sacred intentionality (chapters 3–4). Sacred intentionality is the instrument of resolve toward experiencing a purposeful and guided freedom, self-discipline, moderation, and joy in our dance.

Let's Get Practical

1. For one week in your pop culture journal begin to log your emotional agitations to help you identify your "default modes." Compare your agitations with a friend. Keep track of how your agitations change over time.

2. For one week, practice being more aware of the reason for your pursuit of pop culture. Develop the habit of asking whether the pursuit is associated with "reward," "relief," or "resignation" engagement.

3. Put a sticky note on your phone screen to remind you to look up from your device. During mealtimes, turn off your phone and put it out of sight. Take note of peoples' reactions to your behavior.

4. Select one pop culture distraction today that you are going to deny yourself for the entire day. What did you select and why? At the end of the day, reflect on your experience. What did you learn? Repeat the exercise with a new pop culture distraction.

Discussion Questions

1. What might be the contemporary equivalent of dance marathons?

2. What are your "default modes" when you are bored? What are your "go-to" ways to relieve boredom? What could some alternatives be when it comes to relieving boredom?

3. Do you agree that those three motivations—reward, relief, or resignation—are a prominent part of your media engagement? Are these three motivations exhaustive? Are there other motivations?

4. Do you have times when you are "scrolling for the sake of scrolling"? Why?

SACRED INTENTIONALITY

Chapter 3

Dancing with Sacred Intentionality
(Discovering an Undivided Heart)

"Having taught me one way, give me one heart to walk therein, for too often I feel a heart and a heart, two natures contending, two principles struggling for sovereignty. Our minds are apt to be divided between a variety of objects, like trickling streamlets which waste their force in a hundred runnels; our great desire should be to have all our life-floods poured into one channel and to have that channel directed towards the Lord alone."[1]

**—CHARLES H. SPURGEON, NINETEENTH-CENTURY
ENGLISH PREACHER AND THEOLOGIAN**

"Blessed are the pure in heart, for they will see God."

—MATTHEW 5:8 (NIV)

IN *SCREWTAPE LETTERS*, CHRISTIAN author and apologist C. S. Lewis chronicles a boot camp for devils. The master Screwtape instructs Wormwood, his nephew demon-in-training, on the intricacies of temptation. He explains there are "curiosities so feeble" that Wormwood's "assigned [human] target is only half aware of them."[2] As a result, the target is easily led astray by the endless gratification of essentially nothing. Even feeble curiosities lead to distraction and destruction when humans are intentional only about surviving the dullness of everyday life.

Screwtape identifies the human tendency to be more externally distracted than purposefully directed in life's journey. He suggests that human beings often lack *sacred intentionality*. Our distractions—pop culture or otherwise—are not mindfully connected to the overarching vocation of loving service to God and our neighbor. Instead, they are scattered, fragmented, and often in random pursuit of self-gratification.

> Sacred intentionality connects our pop culture desires to God's call to serve him and love our neighbors.

We often tell our students that our culture's spiritual crucible, its unique test, is best felt during the first sense of boredom's pull. It is that moment when, only listless at first, the discomfort of dissatisfaction with the present activity (e.g., schoolwork, conversation, laundry, lawn care, birdseed replenishment) makes us susceptible to seeking out alleviating distractions. It is almost as if any distraction will do. We further explain how we have conditioned ourselves to be equal-opportunity diversionaries—all of us, professors included. In our bored, listless state, having turned our back on the sacredness of the moment, we typically seek the salvific intervention of mass media and its younger sibling, social media. Basically, our students eventually concede that Screwtape got it right. So, now what?

In Part One of Sacred Intentionality (chapter 3), we explore the following central ideas:

- How the God-given gifts of intentionality and curiosity can be used to cultivate mindful pop culture participation and avoid the "entertain-me-now" expectations that prevent everyday Sabbath rest. We suggest that one's understanding of, and commitment to, ultimate calling is what informs and energizes one's capacity to develop sacred intentionality toward anything in life.

- To further understand curiosity's role in the process, we consider Saint Augustine's fifth-century observations on sacrilegious versus sacred curiosities. How we distinguish between holy and profane curiosities is critical since some curiosities propel us toward healthy and enlivening discoveries while others propel us toward unhealthy, even deadening, ones.

Then, in Part Two (chapter 4), we conclude by demonstrating how being purposeful about our use of discretionary time and making intentional appointments with pop culture can be used as strategies to help develop sacred intentionality. Being purposeful requires the holy habit of discernment, which allows us to be more attentive to the distinctions between wisdom and foolishness. Discernment helps us to recognize what is at stake in each of our pop culture decisions. It also promotes what we describe as "prophetic shock therapy," or a necessary jolt to our everyday, casual way of engaging pop culture that can numb us to the reality of sacred intentionality.

The Common Graces of Intentionality and Curiosity

A driver in Northbridge, Massachusetts, who stated that she did not even like golf, drove her car into a sand trap on a golf course. Northbridge Police explained that her GPS told her to turn left and that this left brought her into a cornfield and once she was in the cornfield, she kept driving, trying to get out of the cornfield. The driver, who blamed her malfunctioning digital navigation system, or GPS, for the mistake, ended up exactly where the car directed her to go, although we suspect she certainly did not intend for her car's final resting place to be the sand trap of a golf course.[3]

Intentionality is the human capacity to deliberately choose one thing over another, one path over another.[4] It is a common grace or a gift of God common to humanity. Intentions provide hints to the largest and smallest "whys" of our existence. Our lives are drenched in meaningful intentions whether we are conscious of them or not.

 INTENTIONALITY

"When the mind with great earnestness, and of choice, fixes its view on any idea, considers it on all sides, and will not be called off by the ordinary solicitation of other ideas, it is that we call intention . . . ."[5]

—John Locke, seventeenth-century British philosopher and physician

Intentionality is a dominant element when choosing and pursuing a career path, or choosing to be faithful to a marital partner, friend, or local church. But it is also a dominant element when, with controller in hand, you fly through 500 programming options or download almost limitless possibilities from your favorite streaming service. The controller finally pauses and selects its option because *you* paused it and settled in. *You* made the selection, maybe only for ten minutes, sometimes for three hours, but in those ten minutes or three hours all other entertainment options are unavailable. In an entertainment-saturated environment that dominates most of our lives, we are regularly making choices, expressing intention. It is a sacred use of intentionality when we tie such choosing to the "calling" bestowed upon us by our Creator.

Intentional living is a lot like a GPS used by many motorists. A GPS requires putting in the right destination and a beginning point. A GPS knows where you are starting your journey. And once you enter a destination, it calculates a path for you to follow. In the same way, intentional living points one toward life's ultimate destination found in Christ Jesus and toward the path found in God's Word. But following a GPS mindlessly and without attention to the nuances and common-sense indicators along the route means we can end up like the Northbridge driver mentioned earlier, a bit off from our intended course, even despite our best and most sacred of intentions.

Curiosity is also God's gift; it requires intentionality; it is never without purpose.

Like intentionality, *curiosity* is a gift of God, a common grace with implications for all of life including our pop culture choices. It is our desire to see something novel or discover something new. Third-century Church Father Origen described curiosity and inquisitiveness as essential to a passion for learning and as a gift of God that leads to academic, artistic, and scientific discovery.[6] Curiosity may be fueled by passion or desire but it still requires an intentional stretching or bending of the mind; some deliberate exertion of one's intellectual faculties toward a particular object.

In addition, curiosity is never without purpose, whether we are aware of it or not. It is driven by intentionality. In other words, curiosity does not generally precede intention but is launched, shaped, and justified by it.

BOREDOM'S CURE

"The cure for boredom is curiosity. There is no cure for curiosity."[7]

—Dorothy Parker, American poet, writer, critic, and satirist

When faithfully stewarded, curiosity is a gateway provocation in the mind, large or small, leading to enthusiasm and passion. It becomes what Puritan theologian Jonathan Edwards called a "spiritual affection," moving the will to act.[8] But as Screwtape reminds us, like all gracious instruments that can be used and misused, curiosity can trigger movement toward the discovery of trivia and personal gratification on the one hand, or profundity and glorious revelation on the other.

Sometimes curiosity is provoked by a lack of stimulation from the three-dimensional circumstances that surround us. It launches off the threshold of discontent and gives permission to explore every pop culture outlet with the self-justification, "I wonder what's on my favorite streaming service, social media site, and whether someone reached out to me in the last seven minutes?" The ancient preacher of Ecclesiastes warns the reader long before the exploding myriad of digital distractions, "Better what the eye sees than the roving of the appetite" (6:9, NIV). But we techno-urban dwellers have become conditioned by the discontentedness with what is in front of us. We are curious. So, we roam, our appetite for novelty causing us to wonder what is in the next room, what treasures await us in the neighbor's house, and just how much greener is the grass on the other side of the fence?

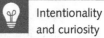

Intentionality and curiosity are sacred when they are guided by who we are committed to be as followers of Jesus Christ.

Curiosity always asks the question that begins with the two words, "I wonder . . . ?" Sometimes it is wise to follow through on our wonderings, and sometimes foolish. The shepherds in the fields that first Christmas evening were curious enough to ask each other on their rushed jaunt to Bethlehem, "I wonder what we'll find?" For certain, not all curiosities are provoked by an angelic visit.

In short, gifts of intentionality and curiosity—and our capacity to be intentional and curious—should never serve as ends to themselves, and when they do we often end up in pop culture cornfields and sand traps. Instead, these gifts' parameters are ideally formed and bounded by allegiance to higher purposes than personal pleasure, relief, or reward-viewing, or any other escape from the banality of our existence. When intentionality and curiosity are guided by who we are committed to be and what we are determined to do in light of the biblical witness, they become sacred. Such sacred intentionality gives purpose and direction to life—including each step in our dance with pop culture—and everything heightens our awareness to the possibility of the sacredness of each and every moment. Sacred intentionality is available to all people to choose life patterns in light of their ultimate calling before God.

SEARCHING FOR THE SACRED

"The reverent among us possess excellent vision. They have trained themselves to see God's Spirit and his handiwork. They know the sacred when they see it, and the sacred is that in which God is found. With a finely tuned lens, there is much to see."[9]

—Gregory Spencer, *Awakening the Quieter Virtues*

Ultimate Calling

One day a farmer observed a peculiar cloud formation while standing in his field. The clouds formed the letters G, P, and C, which he interpreted as a call from God to "Go Preach Christ!" The excited farmer hurried to his church deacons, proclaiming his call to preach. Respectful of his passion, they invited him to preach the following Sunday; his sermon ran over by thirty minutes and was utterly incomprehensible. After the sermon the deacons sat speechless in the presence of the passionate preacher-farmer. "Well?" the farmer asked. After several seconds of silence, the eldest deacon finally spoke up, "Seems to me the clouds were saying 'Go plant corn.'"[10]

This is likely not the first time there has been confusion about what it means to be called by God to do something. The concept of Christian calling is a profound biblical idea, and biblical history is full of stories about calls to faithful servants who put a meaningful stamp on their generation.

For our purposes, when we talk about "calling" we are referring to *ultimate* purposes of existence. A Christian's ultimate calling can be described in various ways. A traditional description found in the *Westminster Confession of Faith* is to glorify God and enjoy him forever. Another is to become more Christ-like in loving service to God and others. Still another is to cultivate our capacity to love sacrificially. Each description adds a layer of meaning and helps picture what it means to live a life of ultimate calling in Christ.[11]

OUR CALLING

"There is no single calling, one-track plan, or changeless career for our lives. Even Abraham's trip to Moriah was just one episode in a life of uncanny ups and downs as well as surprising twists and turns. He was not called merely to a job, profession, or occupation. Abraham was called to obedience, to worship God in every part of his life, from hospitality to marriage to sacrificing his son."[12]

—Quentin J. Schultze, *Here I Am: Now What on Earth Should I Be Doing?*

It is the Bible's audacious testimony that *every* word and deed will be judged that provides context for ultimate calling.[13] The Bible does not back off from its sometimes annoying stridency on this point. It also explains the Apostle Paul's repeated and comprehensive command to do and say *all* things in the name of the Lord Jesus Christ.[14] Meaning saturates everything, from the seemingly mundane to the strikingly profound, as with the many pop culture choices perpetually before us.

LIVING SHALLOW AND DEEP

"To be shallow is not a sign of being sinful, nor is shallowness an indication that there is no depth to your life at all—the ocean has a shore. Even the shallow things of life, such as eating and drinking, walking and talking, are ordained by God. These are all things our Lord did. He did them as the Son of God, and He said, 'A disciple is not above his teacher . . .' (Matt. 10:24). We are safeguarded by the shallow things of life. We have to live the surface, commonsense life in a commonsense way. Then when God gives us the deeper things, they are obviously separated from the shallow concerns."[15]

—Oswald Chambers, *My Utmost for His Highest*

Ultimate calling is the antidote to divided-life spirituality we find as we dance with pop culture.[16] Such spirituality makes traditionally secular categories of life, including business, government, education, and pop culture, submissive to the same sanctifying significance as more traditional spiritual disciplines like Bible study, prayer, meditation, service, and worship. It is why ancient Israel was encouraged to hide the word of the Lord on their hearts. It is why King David joyously proclaimed that he meditated on God's law all day long (Ps. 119:97). It is the lens through which David admonishes his readers, while lying on their beds, to "search your hearts" (Ps. 4:4,

Ultimate calling offers a remedy to a divided-life spirituality.

NIV). Ultimate calling is the fountain that ideally feeds and refreshes all intentions, curiosities, and pursuits, including engagement in mass-mediated entertainments.

Quite frankly, many have no clue about their ultimate calling. Even if they do, it often has little leverage in shaping decisions amidst the flurry of entertainment landscapes and pop culture fare. More than fifty years ago, British author Dorothy Sayers lamented that Western culture was made of humans who "loved nothing, hated nothing, stood for nothing and, in fact, remain alive only because they found nothing for which they could sacrifice, let alone die."[17] Sound familiar? More recently, cultural analyst and theologian Thomas C. Oden described postmodern (and post-Christian) culture as being driven by a "narcissistic hedonism" governed by the over-arching maxim, "[do] whatever makes me feel good now."[18] Some people might confess to a generic altruistic life calling, but it often lacks the kind of convicting grip needed to shape all of life effectively.

BORN TO PLAY

"We are called to be characters in this story, to play the role of God's image bearers who care for and cultivate God's creation, to the praise of his glory. To learn this role is to become what we were made to be. This is not playacting or pretending: it is the role we were born to play. In becoming these characters, we become ourselves. To assume this role is to find our vocation."[19]

—James K. A. Smith, *You Are What You Love: The Spiritual Power of Habit*

For all their strengths and benefits, pop culture platforms—and our occasionally unintentional approach toward them—are frequently the oceans that drown our commitment to ultimate calling. We desire to serve others, but too often mindlessly use our discretionary time to check our

How does your ultimate calling specifically inform your pop culture engagement?

online status or view our favorite show's latest episode. Our friend is in crisis but we unthinkingly use the next hour to post messages or surf the web. We habitually approach discretionary time with no real sense (or at least awareness) of our ultimate calling before God. We boldly set sail in pop culture seas without first tying our mooring line to life's ultimate dock. No wonder we tend to drift aimlessly.

So how is your pop culture engagement *specifically* informed by your ultimate calling? This question can be phrased in a slightly different way: who are you resolved to *be* and, subsequently, what are you resolved to *do* in light of your Christian calling?

A crisis of our befuddled and perpetually distracted culture is an inability (or unwillingness?) to answer this question. But if we do not, then it is difficult to identify things that distract us. And if we do not know what we are distracted from, then how can we call anything a distraction at all?

The challenge for followers of Jesus Christ is to be persistent with our ultimate calling despite the myriad of competing voices and distractions vying for our attention. Even as ultimate calling is clarified, the calling will naturally melt into the competing cultural soup if our ultimate calling is not regularly retrieved, reasserted, and practiced in our normal, everyday living. Or as Saint Augustine suggests in the section that follows, curiosities can quickly turn from sacred to sacrilegious when ultimate calling is ignored.

 RESISTANCE IS YOUR DUTY

"As soon as principles that are contrary to your deepest convictions gain ground, then resistance is your duty and acquiescence a sin."[20]

—Abraham Kuyper, nineteenth-century Dutch journalist, philosopher, and theologian

Sacrilegious and Sacred Curiosities

Saint Augustine appeared to have some problems with curiosity back in the fourth century. Basically, he was the ultimate party animal in hot pursuit of personal pleasures. Describing his life prior to conversion he notes, "I wasted myself away in great sin. I followed in the path of *sacrilegious curiosity* [italics ours], allowing it to lead me, in my desertion of [God], down to the depths of infidelity."[21] What might Augustine mean by "sacrilegious curiosity"?

It appears that Augustine divided the concept of curiosity into two categories: sacrilegious curiosity and, by implication, sacred curiosity. *Sacred curiosities* are those that uphold God's exaltedness, and we are wise to pursue them. *Sacrilegious curiosities* are profane because they show irreverence toward the sacred. Fools pursue such curiosities.

A NOSE FOR THE PROFANE

"The profane sounds ugly, as it should. The profane is that which intentionally dismisses, ridicules, or destroys the sacred. Standing up to the profane means that we notice what breaks the heart of God and that we resist it. To put it another way, a nose for the profane sniffs out what smells to high heaven."[22]

—Gregory Spencer, *Awakening the Quieter Virtues*

Wise and foolish paths are familiar images from the Bible. Yet how do we wisely distinguish between sacred and sacrilegious curiosities? What curiosities propel us toward healthy and enlivening discoveries and which ones propel us toward unhealthy, deadening realizations?

One clue is found in the Bible's emphasis on both selfish and unselfish ambition. Ambition comes from the Latin *ambitio,* meaning soliciting votes or lobbying for something. *Selfish* ambition is what fuels campaigning for self, as in self-promotion. It seeks great things for oneself—e.g., money, recognition, power, prestige, status, and pleasure—without regard for others and is condemned in Scripture. In James 3:16 the epistle's author even describes selfish ambition as a dominant cause of "disorder and every evil practice" (NIV). In contrast, *unselfish* ambition allows us to be energized about our present and future within the context of serving and promoting others.[23]

AMBITION'S CHARACTER

"It is motivation that determines ambition's character. Our Lord never taught against the urge to high achievement, but He did expose and condemn unworthy motivation."[24]

—J. Oswald Sanders, *Spiritual Leadership*

Curiosity can be understood in similar ways. Just as ambition can be selfish or unselfish, humane or inhumane, curiosity can be employed to serve beyond merely self-absorbed ends. For instance, our curiosity not only fuels medical and scientific discoveries that help others but also fuels a desire to view a particular play or movie, read a particular short story, attend an art exhibit, or create a new app or website that offers wisdom and insight that benefit others.

Our sacred use of curiosity can also provoke greater relational depth, whether it is with God or our neighbor. A desire to know someone better, more deeply, respectfully, and clearly is partially launched by curiosity. Finding out more about how we may serve them, the wisdom we can glean, or how we may be more faithful in our friendships is an outworking of sacred curiosity.

 A SPIRITUALLY VIGOROUS SAINT

"A spiritually vigorous saint never believes that his circumstances simply happen at random, nor does he ever think of his life as being divided into the secular and the sacred. A saint is not to take the initiative toward self-realization, but toward knowing Jesus Christ. He sees every situation in which he finds himself as the means of obtaining a greater knowledge of Jesus Christ, and he has an attitude of unrestrained abandon and total surrender about him. The Holy Spirit is determined that we will have the realization of Jesus Christ in every area of our lives, and He will bring us back to the same point over and over again until we do."[25]

—Oswald Chambers, *My Utmost for His Highest*

In his journey toward a more unified vision and experience of allegiance to God, Saint Augustine lamented, "being turned away from you, the One, I lost myself in the distractions of the Many."[26] He was drained of rest. Mentally, physically, and spiritually exhausted by his pursuit of entertainments and pleasure, triggered by his sacrilegious curiosities. Augustine prayed for an undivided set of desires, loves, and longings, always aware of God's presence and call to holiness and wisdom. Such desires included his entertainment longings and passions for novelty. Augustine was certainly on target. In the undivided heart, there is no desire, no curiosity, no longing or love, no aspiration or dream allowed free rein, except as informed by our guided freedom in the Lord.[27]

 Having undivided desires means that we are constantly aware of God's call to holiness and wisdom in every moment.

By reflecting on pop culture's relation to ultimate calling, one can learn the habit of hearing and seeing the sacred amidst our culture's cacophony of rival voices and images. We can learn the wisdom of approaching pop culture with sacred intentionality, identifying other available dances that help promote salvation, justice, and peace.

Conclusion

Though written during World War II, fifteen years prior to the conquest of television and half a century before the personal computer, *Screwtape Letters* speaks loudly to our pop culture dance today. It draws attention to the powerful efficiency of trivial nothings fueled by feeble curiosities that separate us from sacred intentionality and allegiance to God.

Intentionality becomes sacred as it is mindfully contextualized by the general vocation of the believer to become more Christ-like, our ultimate calling.[28] In this light, our thoughts, our words, and our actions—including our interactions with pop culture—can contribute to true human flourishing and *shalom*.

> Intentionality becomes sacred when it is driven by a desire to become more Christ-like.

In our next chapter, we focus on how we can further discern between sacrilegious and sacred curiosities. With impoverished discernment, we end up turning wisdom and foolishness upside down. As we develop discernment, we imitate God as moral beings who take responsibility for their life's choices, including pop culture choices. Choosing wisdom in the little pop culture moments of our life prepares us for choosing wisdom in more monumental situations.

Let's Get Practical

1. In your pop culture journal, spend at least one week tracking your "discretionary time" and how it is spent. Avoid premature judgments—your focus at the end of the day is to record how many minutes or hours were deemed "discretionary." What did you learn? Record your observations in your pop culture journal.

2. For one day, intentionally allow yourself not to follow the crowd in seeing the latest movie, viral video sensation, or latest episode of everyone's favorite television program. How did it make you feel? What other dances did you participate in? Enter your reflections in your pop culture journal.

3. For one day (or an entire week), record each of your pop culture engagements. Be specific, including the amount of time spent with each. Then, at the end of the day (or week), reflect on these questions in light of your choices: How do my pop culture choices reflect who I am resolved to *be* and, subsequently, what I am resolved to *do* in light of my Christian calling?

Discussion Questions

1. How is the common grace of "curiosity" both a blessing and curse in your life?

2. How do we know when acting on our curiosity is wise and when it is foolish?

3. What are the intentions that inform your curiosities? Does your pursuit of this or that curiosity serve only yourself, or does it potentially serve others?

Chapter 4

Abandoning Sacrilegious Curiosities
(The Holy Habit of Discernment)

"Woe to those who call evil good and good evil, who put dark-
ness for light and light for darkness, who put bitter for sweet
and sweet for bitter."

—ISAIAH 5:20 (NIV)

"Seeing reality for what it is is what we call discernment.
The work of discernment is very hard."[1]

—LEWIS B. SMEDES, TWENTIETH-CENTURY
THEOLOGIAN AND ETHICIST

IN HIS SERMON ON the Mount (Matt. 5–7), Jesus asserts metaphorically
that everyone is building a house because everyone is building a life. Those
who apply his teachings from the Sermon on the Mount are wisely building
their house on rock; those who do not are foolishly building their house on
sand. His parable makes it clear that storms and floods assault both types of
houses. Yet, the significance of Jesus's insights about living wisely provides
the solid foundation for a life prepared to face inevitable tests and trials.
Building the house requires the intentionality of the builder, especially
the intentional choosing of the building's foundation. The Lord asks his

Sacred curiosities uphold God's character. Sacrilegious ones mock it.

original audience just getting nestled into the hillside, and definitely amazed by what they are hearing, "Just what kind of house do you intend on building?" In other words, who are you intending to become?

Our point is that the gift of intentionality is designed by God as a necessary tool in the dance of life. Intentionality is the ability to discern—and then choose—life-affirming dances over self-destructive ones, sacred curiosities over sacrilegious ones. We can intentionally cultivate wisdom or folly, just as we can intentionally build a house with a strong foundation or a weak one. We can choose a path and persist on it despite the temptations to waiver, despite the occasional avalanche of distractions, barriers, and reversals. We can purposefully choose day to day, and even moment to moment, a promised land of greater wisdom and deeper love. We can defy the facade of the randomness of existence, which, if not confronted, can hurl us toward ultimate anxieties of purposelessness. This ability to intend, to choose, is to be celebrated as a gift of God to all people.

It is this kind of intentionality that should certainly be true of our dance with pop culture. In reconsidering our dance, we begin to ask ourselves: Are we choosing wisely, prudently, skillfully, carefully, thoughtfully, and joyfully when it comes to our pop culture choices? We can intentionally learn the habit of being more attentive to the voice of God. Such attentiveness cultivates discernment, or the ability to draw accurate conclusions about what is in front of us. And practicing discernment is at the heart of who we are as imager bearers and imitators of Christ. By practicing discernment, we can learn the wisdom of selecting dances and dance partners that are consistent with our God-given role as exultant creatures.

So Many Different Dances

As discussed in our previous chapter, to lead our dance with sacred intentionality we must take seriously the Bible's call to redeem our time considering our ultimate calling, not merely to kill it. This redemption begins with a shift in the way we process our discretionary time choices. As we do this, we can experience a pop culture complemented life, not a pop culture dominated one. To aid in this shift, it

Ultimate calling helps us to avoid a pop culture-dominated life that interferes with Sabbath rest.

is helpful to ponder other dance categories often marginalized and sometimes bullied by our primary pop culture affections and boredom default modes. Each of the following categories is also a dance, offering opportunities to learn the wise rhythms of its joys.

Family/Friend Dance

This dance involves the option of initiating contact with anyone in your sphere of relationships who enables human health, social, and spiritual well-being. Just as any support system requires maintenance to function effectively, family and friendships require investments of time and energy to maintain and strengthen them.

 "Greater love has no one than this: to lay down one's life for one's friends" (John 15:13, NIV).

As with any dance, if one or both dance partners are inexperienced and not paying attention, damage can be done. Sometimes our engagement with family and friends leaves us with sore toes and bruised shins. And rarely does anyone want to dance out of obligation, which is why we would much prefer to try our luck with ninety minutes of online messaging and why some of us would even prefer a virtually constructed Second Life.[2]

But the Scriptures assert that part of a faithful existence as God's image-bearers involves the obligation—yes, obligation—to family and friends. Certainly, the Ten Commandments make clear the responsibility to honor our mother and father. The prophet Isaiah says that true fasting should not include "a turn away from your own flesh and blood" (58:7, NIV). The book of Proverbs asserts that "a friend loves at all times, and a brother is born for a time of adversity" (17:17, NIV).

SEDUCTIVE TECHNOLOGY

"Technology is seductive when what it offers meets our human vulnerabilities. And as it turns out, we are very vulnerable indeed. We are lonely but fearful of intimacy. Digital connections and the sociable robot may offer the illusion of companionship without the demands of friendship. Our networked life allows us to hide from each other, even as we are tethered to each other. We'd rather text than talk."[3]

—Sherry Turkle, *Alone Together: Why We Expect More from Technology and Less from Each Other*

The discretionary time before us often overlooks the importance of investing in these central support systems. Sometimes in our exhausted or self-entitled state, the least welcome interruptions come from the responsibilities inherent in family life and friendships. Yet the initiated conversations and activities with friends and family—even the invitations to join us in mass-mediated entertainment fare—are the investments that pay rich dividends in deepening the graces of our life. Part of being a friend is being someone who loves at all times, and it is something that provides deepening context for serving family members in times of adversity. Regularly choosing to strengthen your relational support system instead of defaulting to entertainment longings will assist in making sure that this dance option is not bullied by pop culture's easy accessibility.

THE ESSENCE OF HOSPITALITY

"Hospitality, therefore, means primarily the creation of a free space where the stranger can enter and become a friend instead of an enemy. Hospitality is not to change people, but to offer them space where change can take place. It is not to bring men and women over to our side, but to offer freedom not disturbed by dividing lines."[4]

—Henri J. M. Nouwen, *Reaching Out: The Three Movements of the Spiritual Life*

Service-Ministry Dance

This dance involves the option of initiating ministry based upon the common-good impulse—that is, caring for the sick, visiting the prisoner or the distressed, the infirmed.[5] The term "ministry" is not restricted to the work reserved for professional clergy but speaks to everyone's responsibility to care for those in need.

This, too, is a necessary dance requiring both an unselfish willingness and persistent wisdom. The willingness to serve others in need is a significant privilege and a necessary aspect of functioning fully. Wisdom in this dance also involves awareness of the energy exerted and the recuperation time required. Just ask someone involved in caring long-term for a loved one.

Jesus's life certainly involved service to others beyond his friends and family. Mark's Gospel tells us that our Savior did not come to be served, but to serve, and to give his life as ransom for others (10:45). Too often we

SAINT BASIL'S WISDOM

"The bread in your cupboard belongs to the hungry man; the coat hanging unused in your closet belongs to the man who needs it; the shoes rotting in your closet belong to the man who has no shoes; the money which you put into the bank belongs to the poor. You do wrong to everyone you could help but fail to help."[6]

—Saint Basil of Caesarea, fourth-century Church Father

would rather yield to our entertainment impulses than spend time with this alternative dance. Yet we are wired to function most fully when we are actively involved in helping meet the needs not just of family and friends but also of those beyond the familiar confines of relational comfort. It is a certain antidote to narcissism and selfish ambition.

One additional benefit of this ministerial dance is the cultivation of our empathetic capacity. This includes the ability to feel as others feel, to put ourselves in their shoes, to "rejoice with those who rejoice; mourn with those who mourn," as the Apostle Paul describes in Romans 12:15 (NIV).

THE EMPATHY PARADOX

Research by the University of Michigan's Institute for Social Research (ISR) reports an empathy paradox of increasing disconnection in the age of increasing connection. The ISR analyzing data on empathy among 14,000 college students over the last thirty years found a 47 percent drop in their empathy index, much of it in the last decade. "A contradictory portrait it is," says media critic Clifford G. Christians: "High connectivity for the Wi-Fi generation and low connectivity in terms of emotional concern for others."[7]

This dance option typically requires some planning ahead, which is part of the problem since it does not take much planning to snatch an hour or two of our favorite pop culture delight. But prisoners cannot always be visited at our convenience. The sick and the dying cannot always be contacted on a whim. Our friend Mary schedules her nursing home visits weeks in advance. Residents wait with great anticipation for her arrival and beam with delight when she finally walks through the door. There is simply no app that replaces the relational power of Mary's physical presence with nursing home residents.

Artistic-Athletic Dance

This dance is triggered by an impulse for creative work and thought or athletic development. For instance, a poem is refined, a song is composed, or an athletic skill is practiced, especially when there is nothing formally scheduled or institutionally mandated that triggers the activity.

 THE ARTIST'S JOB

"But [mass entertainment is] the opposite of art because the job of mass entertainment is to cajole, seduce and flatter consumers to let them know that what they thought was right is right, and that their tastes and their immediate gratification are of the utmost concern of the purveyor. The job of the artist, on the other hand, is to say, wait a second, to the contrary, everything we have thought is wrong. Let's reexamine it."[8]

—David Mamet, author and playwright

Often, our invitation to athletic activities and exercise is regimented by strict practice schedules and seasonal dictates. When was the last time you extemporaneously contacted someone to toss the football around, shoot baskets, or play nine holes of golf? Such activities can become habits during discretionary time if they are regularly engaged, functionally accessible, and especially if you can experience some success.

Artistic expression can also include manual labor such as planting a garden or building something. We consider ourselves amateur carpenters and enjoy building dog houses, bird houses, and, in one case, a bookshelf wall where one of the shelves is a door to a hidden room.

Our friend Charlie called us recently to schedule a game of doubles tennis at the campus courts. Ironically, we were in the middle of our own entertainment entitlement when he called. With our wives' encouragement we met up at the courts for a time of exercise and fellowship. Between points we chatted about family, students, and personal struggles. It was an opportunity to engage in something beyond spectator passivity.

Devotional Life Dance

This dance option includes spiritual disciplines such as prayer, Bible study, and meditation, to name a few, and is often experienced in solitude. Sometimes it is referred to as "quiet time with God." Our Lord's commitment to the habit of a devotional dance with his Father often required solitude. He carved out time to recharge his interior life after the demands of his disciples for instruction and the cries of the crowds for miracles. We are thus wise to regularly set aside time to deepen our intimacy with God.

But along with the Psalmist (Ps. 16:8), our Lord would also assert the constant presence of his Father. So, in emphasizing that our devotional time is "time with God," we can unduly minimize the sacredness of other categories of activity and thought, including our dance with pop culture. Our dance with pop culture should also be considered "time with God," and even an act of worship.

 ## SPIRITUAL DISCIPLINE

"The concept of the spiritual disciplines is really quite simple: we do the practices that Jesus did. Over time these practices become habitual, thus enabling us to respond to life in a way more like Jesus would if he were to live our life. As we submit our will to spiritual practices, God's grace brings forth character transformation. This seems to be the dominant means God uses to bring about change in our lives. Christian spiritual formation is the process of becoming people formed into the likeness of Christ's character."[9]

—Nathan Foster, *The Making of an Ordinary Saint*

Imagine you are sitting in a comfortable chair reading a graphic novel or watching your favorite movie. You read a sentence or watch a scene that shakes you deeply. Perhaps it prompts you to ponder the deep meaning of a certain word, like *love, humility,* or *forgiveness.* Then, imagine putting down the book or turning off the movie, getting up from your chair, and doing a topical Bible study on love, humility, or forgiveness. How often do these kinds of devotional moments occur during or after we are immersed in a pop culture moment? But this kind of mindful devotional activity allows us to treat pop culture interaction as a spiritually formative, devotional practice, and not just entertainment.

WONDERFUL SILENCE

"It is in this silent state that [one] communicates with God. Silence becomes both a wonderful transmission and receiving of divine communication."[10]

—Jeanne Marie Bouvier de la Motte Guyon, seventeenth-century Catholic mystic

In addition, the devotional dance category is the one often mistakenly used as a barometer of spiritual health. Sometimes when asked how we are doing spiritually, we are conditioned to immediately refer to our devotional life only. This is like asking an athlete how she is doing in her sport and she answers by referring to her healthy eating and exercise regimens. Though these are aspects of athletic excellence, the main answer comes from the athletic arena itself. For the Christian, the main arena serving as a barometer of spiritual health is interpersonal relationships, which can be gauged by the fruit of the Spirit (Gal. 5:22–23).

In short, our point in discussing these four different dance categories is not to elevate one dance over the other but only to assert that for many of us the pop culture dance dominates as a default mode in our discretionary time. When we consciously organize our lives to include different dances during discretionary time, we thwart the dominance of the entertain-me impulse of our dance with pop culture and strengthen our sacred intentionality.

We readily admit that there is some overlap and blending among the four dance categories listed above, and a particular category might also be part of one's specific profession. For example, scriptwriters and film scholars might be "working" while viewing films; some clergy are "on the clock" as they spend time strengthening their devotional lives; and artists may be working around the clock to meet a commissioned deadline. These are hardly discretionary options.

> Alternative dances have in common their desire to find Sabbath rest away from pop culture's dance floor.

Finally, we recognize that the four different dance categories have in common their willingness to seek (and find) everyday Sabbath rest *away* from pop culture's dance floor. Yet there are times when we may rightly and intentionally choose to step onto the dance floor to find Sabbath rest. Making intentional appointments with pop culture is one way to do this.

Making Intentional Appointments with Pop Culture

In our growing commitment to promote sacred intentionality, we started with a seemingly simple exercise. For two weeks we consumed no pop culture unless we first made an intentional appointment with it. We avoided any other spur-of-the-moment pop culture encounters to alleviate our boredom. If bored, we opted for one of the other dances described in the previous section. We set appointed times each day to check our email and voice mail so we could still do our jobs. We held each other accountable at the end of the day. We left room for family emergencies or other work crises.

> 💡 Intentional appointments require us to choose which pop culture options *not* to consume at any given moment.

After two days we were a bit agitated. We felt we were missing something important or falling behind, what is now popularly referred to as FOMO ("Fear of Missing Out"). We also felt spiritually pious when asked to explain what we were doing.

When it was time for our first scheduled appointment with television, we wondered if one hour would turn into two or three, the same way that eating one more potato chip turns into devouring the whole bag. We came prepared with a set of basic questions to help us stay focused and "enact" sacred intentionality.

❓ ENACTING SACRED INTENTIONALITY

1. How does this show help me understand who I am to be and what I am resolved to do as a Jesus follower?

2. What can I take away from this pop culture encounter that helps me communicate more faithfully with God, self, and neighbor?

3. Would I recommend this pop culture dance to someone else, and why or why not?

About twenty minutes into our scheduled programs our minds were spinning. There were so many thoughts related to each question that we could not keep them straight. We decided to keep a pop culture journal (which you have seen us mention in the practical application section at the end of each chapter of this book). We did not worry about the length of each entry but made sure to journal after every appointment. We started adding to our journals throughout the week. We logged the whats, whens, and how-longs of each appointment. We explored reasons behind our choices and

Intentional appointments have the potential to produce freedom and rest.

wondered why we longed so desperately at times to check our smart phones, email, or box scores from last night's game. After one week we looked back to see if we could notice any patterns in our choices. The experience was much like keeping a food journal to help a person develop healthy eating habits. By the time the two weeks ended, our agitation had significantly decreased, and we were ready to debrief with students and colleagues. At least two key themes emerged during discussion: freedom and rest.

First, we experienced *freedom* from the sometimes dominating, overarching demands of our pop culture impulses. With this freedom came a sense of empowerment, as if we were no longer being dragged unwillingly around the dance floor by our pop culture partner. We had more time to do things around the house that had been neglected, hang out with family, and become more involved at church.

Second, although it took a while, we actually experienced *rest*. Interestingly, it was a similar kind of rest to what we experienced with the other discretionary dances listed earlier in this chapter. As we journaled, we realized it was an experience of *rest through resistance*. We resisted the impulse to engage in self-entitlement, relief-, reward-, and resignation-viewing. We resisted the tyranny of our culture's want-more-need-more-now mantra. We were learning to lead the dance. No trance dancing this time around. In the process, our new habit of "appointment-only" viewing helped us realize our (1) patterns of unproductive boredom, and (2) our tendency to alleviate boredom—or any emotional agitation—through the myriad of pop culture choices that dominated our lives. Such alleviation is hardly a cycle that breeds redemptive passion for godly service.

BE ALL THERE

"Wherever you are, be all there."[11]

—Jim Elliot, Christian missionary and martyr

The God-given ability to be intentional is also a dominant element in well-known biblical passages that invite the audience of whatever millennium to choose one of two life paths. Deuteronomy 30:15–20 lays out the two paths of obedience and disobedience, and strongly asserts that such a choice (the starting block of intention) is indeed a matter of life and death.

As part of Joshua's farewell speech to the nation of Israel a generation later, he rallies the people by appealing to their ability to choose between the way of God and the pattern of idols: "Choose for yourselves this day whom you will serve ..." (Josh. 24:15, NIV). Of course, such large, significant decisions are to inform the daily, seemingly less ultimate ones.

 "ABSENT PRESENCE"

"Without laserlike focusing energy we suffer from what sociologists call 'absent presence.' Physically present we may be, but our attention drifts and pinballs, seldom in the here and now."[12]

—Leonard Sweet, *Nudge: Awakening Each Other to the God Who's Already There*

These biblical passages are reframed in the book of Proverbs, inviting the reader to choose between the pathways of wisdom and foolishness. A good percentage of Proverbs, in fact, not only lays out the importance of choosing wisdom as a life goal and personal characteristic but creates vivid pictures of day-to-day decisions that are informed by the meta-choices, the ultimate choices between wisdom and folly. Our choices, whatever the size or significance, contribute to the construction project that is our life.

 Intentional appointments allow us to practice choosing between wisdom and foolishness.

Prophetic Shock Therapy

The kind of intentional appointments with media described above can function as a form of "prophetic shock therapy."[13] When properly planned and stewarded, they can jolt us out of our deeply-rooted habits of complacency and inattentiveness toward the numbing effects of pop culture on our pursuit of purposeful living.

The Hebrew prophets' no-holds-barred confrontations with the status quo were designed to shock the complacent kings, priests, and people out of their numbness toward the dulling effects of destructive habits. The prophets prodded and often shocked their audiences toward reconciliation with God in an attempt to stimulate their moral imagination toward a better way of intentional thinking, doing, and being. Some pop culture can certainly do just that.

SHOUT IT OUT!

" . . . to the hard of hearing you shout, and for the almost blind you draw large and startling figures."[14]

—Flannery O'Connor, Christian novelist and essayist

The prophet's pronouncements and pleas—whether packaged in Jeremiah's straightforward sermons or Ezekiel's street theater or Hosea's mocking satire—pushed the people to see a three-act pattern to their lives and community. This pattern remains today: you were married to God and bound to him in covenant, you have wandered from his care in rebellion, and God is persistently inviting you to return to his arms. To perceive such a purposeful pattern in life provides "tremendous moral power."[15]

In our decision about which pop culture program or artifact to consume, we can exercise sacred intentionality that reinforces a healthy dose of prophetic shock. For instance, there is "shock art" that points directly to social injustices in the world caused by humanity's rebellion against God. Simply look at the horrors of some traditional paintings on this theme: Michelangelo's (1475–1564) *The Last Judgment* (in the Sistine Chapel) or Hieronymus Bosch's (c. 1450–1516) *The Garden of Early Delights*. Bosch's painting depicts a world where humans suffer the chilling consequences of their bad choices. This kind of art certainly convicts, but before it convicts it shocks.[16]

Or consider music like Peter Gabriel's compelling track, "Big Time." The song mocks the significance that our culture places on hitting the big time, reaching fame, or celebrity. In the "big city," sings Gabriel, there is so much stuff we can own; and we can pray to our "big god" while kneeling in our big places of worship. In the video, Gabriel appears to be in a robot-like haze as he pokes fun at the bigger-is-better mantra, even enlarging his mouth to ensure that his oversized words come out right. In the song's chorus, the audience is invited to witness its own ridiculous devotion to proof of progress and conspicuous consumption as the song's title phrase is repeated over and over again.[17]

Steve Taylor's song "Cash Cow (A Rock Opera in Three Small Acts)" echoes Gabriel's

> Prophetic shock therapy prompts us to reconsider our commitment to consumerism as a source of contentment. It also calls us to promote racial and economic equality in all its forms.

prophetic tone toward North America's lust for stuff. Taylor's song mocks the prowling "golden Cash Cow"—that is, the golden calf of Exodus 32, essentially now all grown up—and our culture's addiction to material goods. The Cash Cow roams the local shopping mall looking for "proud mortals" to devour—telling them that he loves them, and that he is willing to offer them "good credit" so they can purchase all the creature comforts they deserve. The music video includes grotesque clay-animated characters with deformed, expressionless faces. Taylor's lyrics, performed over ominous Gregorian-like chants at times, confronts our culture's prevailing framing story that says the "good life" is based on what we consume, not who we are as individuals created in God's image.

Pop culture's potential therapeutic shock is not a justification to consume or critique anything under the guise of a redemptive experience. Even truthfulness as the ultimate intention cannot stand without the quality of loving regard for one's neighbor, which means avoiding unethical humor or content that compromises one's moral commitments to sexual purity and nonviolence. The prophets' communication was not driven by animosity toward their community or condescension toward foreigners or enemies of Israel, but by a deep sense of compassion and concern for humanity's plight. Ours should be driven by the same motivations.

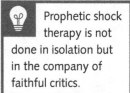

Prophetic shock therapy is not done in isolation but in the company of faithful critics.

Finally, to promote faithful media stewardship, prophetic shock therapy—before and after the fact—must be shared with a company of critics for processing and discernment. This means a humble willingness to process the critique of others. In so doing, we are reminded, just like Elijah was reminded, that bearing witness to the truth, even in ways that provoke shock and anger, never leaves the prophet completely alone.[18] To the extent that we demonstrate such accountability, we practice faithful prophetic shock therapy that helps to foster sacred intentionality.

Conclusion

Jesus's wrap-up to the Sermon on the Mount—the wise and foolish lifetime construction projects—sometimes appears overly simple and void of nuance. Our contemporary self-justification systems naturally push back against the notions of life's legacies and end results being either wise or

> Every pop culture choice gives us an opportunity to practice choosing wisdom over foolishness.

foolish. Yet Jesus, like the patriarchs before him, is pressing his audience, including his twenty-first century audience, not to be immobilized by the flurry of distractions. The call to choose between "two roads" helps to fully orb the biblical vision of significance in every moral choice, including the flurry of choices triggered by discretionary time and income, all of them ideally fueled by sacred intentionality.

Our next chapter explores the second of our *Three Sacreds*, sacred interiority or the cultivation of a deepening thought life through the regular restatement and memorization of guiding biblical principles and truths. Sacred interiority contributes to a wise sense of intentionality toward all of life's dances, including our dance with pop culture.

Let's Get Practical

1. In closing his Sermon on the Mount, Jesus notes that "everyone who hears these words of mine and puts them into practice is like a wise man who built his house on the rock" (Matt. 7:24, NIV). On a blank sheet of paper or digital document, try to list as many of the principles taught by Jesus in his sermon—the truths upon which we are to build our "house." Record them in your journal.

2. Spend one week focusing on cultivating exposure to a different dance that is lacking in your life. Then, next week, pick another dance. In one month, you will cover all four different dances. Lather, rinse, repeat each month. Find your groove.

3. Spend some time pre-arranging two to three pop culture "appointments"—a movie, television program, YouTube documentary, or other pop culture offering. Ideally, invite a family member or friend to experience the encounter with you. Experiment with predetermining what you are going to experience (i.e., How did you come up with your selection? When will you be watching/listening and with whom?).

4. This exercise is about being more engaged in arenas and stories where you have some potential to shape the outcome. Spend thirty minutes listing the people who are part of your own "pastoral care circle." This is anyone in your family, friendship group, or at least two to three

people who are in greater need than you. This will probably be a list of five to twelve people. Begin in a balanced and simple way to initiate prayers and care for one or two people per day. In your journal, keep a list of your pastoral initiatives, social media check-ups and check-ins, phone calls, and notes of encouragement. Record the blessings. Ask tough questions.

Discussion Questions

1. Do you think the pop culture dance is a dominant default mode in your discretionary time? Why or why not?

2. Which of the other "dances" listed in this chapter are most familiar and which are the least familiar? Are there additional "dances" you would add to the list presented?

3. Which one or two of the other "dances" in this chapter are the most compelling to further cultivate in your own spiritual life? Which one(s) are the least compelling to develop?

4. Which of the other "dances" would be easiest for you to strengthen? Which ones would be the most difficult for you to strengthen?

SACRED INTERIORITY

Chapter 5

Dancing with Sacred Interiority
(Calling on God's Truths)

"You brood of vipers, how can you who are evil say anything good?
For the mouth speaks what the heart is full of."

—JESUS SPEAKING IN MATTHEW 12:34 (NIV)

"Above all else, guard your heart, for everything you do flows from it."

—PROVERBS 4:23 (NIV)

IN 1668, TWENTY-SIX-YEAR-OLD WILLIAM Penn—early Quaker and founder of Pennsylvania—sat as a prisoner in the Tower of London, incarcerated by King Charles II for his defiance of preaching restrictions imposed by the Church of England. Penn was given paper and pen to write his confession after which he would be quickly released. Instead, filled with courage and conviction, Penn wrote the now classic tract "No Cross, No Crown." This work was remarkable for its keen historical analysis and citation of 400 biblical passages and 68 authors whose quotations and commentary Penn was able to call to memory without any reference material.[1]

Penn's experience may be difficult, even impossible, to imagine today. Few of us will ever be locked in towers or deprived of our data-rich devices for very long. The Internet is a massive pipeline of never-ending

What is the cost of our never-ending, readily accessible flow of information and entertainment on our spiritual formation?

information and entertainment quickly available at our fingertips that has the potential to enrich our lives. But at what cost?

Despite its obvious benefits, what our over-dependence on the Internet seems to be doing, to some degree, is locking us away in new kinds of isolation towers by chipping away at our capacity for robust contemplation and reprogramming our use of memory. Over time our hyperactive need for data spreads our minds wide and shallow rather than deep. Immersed in the seemingly infinite capacity and permanency of digital culture, we confuse storage with memory and learn to prefer the ease and immediacy of our "outboard brain."[2] In the process, we unintentionally hinder our capacity to cultivate *sacred interiority*, or the experience of a faithful and deepening interior thought life that provides a wellspring of creativity and from which we may call to mind the contextualizing truths that give meaning to all of life.

In Part One of Sacred Interiority (chapter 5), we explore the following key ideas:

- How cultivating a healthy sacred interiority can strengthen one's ability to resist even the slightest form of what we call *technological idolatry* and living a shallow life. Over time, our expanding interiority can instill a deepening sacredness that aims to conform to the mind of Christ in every one of life's dances, including our dance with pop culture.[3]

- How the deepening and broadening of our sacred interiority begins with a decision to identify what is worth remembering and then choosing to do the mental work of "writing it on the tablets of your heart" (Prov. 7:3, NIV).[4] Several biblical examples that illustrate the importance of building a substantive interior life will be highlighted.

Then, in Part Two (chapter 6) we conclude by unfolding a strategy for enhancing one's capacity for sacred interiority, a process we call "stewarding the stirrings of the soul." We explain how turning attention to our stored sacred wisdom—the words of Christ and the apostles, the psalms, the patriarchs, church mothers and fathers, or anything that inspires us to wisdom and spiritual victory—is an immediate escape from the mental turmoil of envy, lust, and worry.

Living in the Shallows

With the deluge of information available to us from so many places, including e-readers and tablets, it is very likely we read more today than we did decades ago. But it is a "different kind of reading," and "behind it lies a different kind of thinking—perhaps even a new sense of the self."[5]

ADVANTAGE, PRINT

When screen reading, we are less likely to take part in metacognitive learning regulation, which includes strategies such as setting specific goals, re-reading difficult portions, or checking our understanding as we go. In one study, students took multiple-choice exams about expository texts either on computers or on paper. Half the students were limited to seven minutes of study time; the other half could review the text for as long as they liked. When pressured to read quickly, screen readers and paper readers performed equally well. But when managing study time, paper readers scored 10 percentage points higher. Paper readers presumably approached the exam with a more studious mind-set than screen-readers and more effectively directed their attention and working memory.[6]

In the Internet age, our thinking has become somewhat hyper-textual as we struggle to pay attention to longer forms of writing—or longer forms of anything for that matter. Thought life takes on a choppy quality that mirrors the way we quickly scan multiple online sources. Our minds expect to consume information in the same way the Web sends it out: in a fast, mercurial moving stream of bits and bytes. "Once I was a scuba diver in the sea of words," explains award-winning author Nicholas Carr. "Now I zip along the surface like a guy on a Jet Ski."[7]

There is little doubt that the Internet is changing our brains, including our memory. Our use of search engines and handheld devices makes it rather easy for us to forget to remember. Few of us can recall the last time we had to memorize someone's phone number or email address. Researchers report that when people know that information will be stored on a computer, they are less likely to remember it (although they are better at remembering *where* this information was stored).[8] Our short-term memory, which transfers information to long-term memory and makes deeper mental processing possible, is especially vulnerable since its limited storage capacity is easily swept clean by the Internet's frequent breaks in our attention.

PHOTO-TAKING IMPAIRMENT EFFECT

Taking photos—an ever-present activity in our smartphone-addicted culture—may interfere with our ability to remember the very objects we photograph, something called the photo-taking impairment effect. When we count on technology to remember for us, we do not attend fully or internalize the events we capture with our cameras.[9]

Moreover, our use of the term *memory* to describe information storage is a bit odd since computers do not have the ability to select, which is a basic feature of memory. Rather than dealing with a simple problem of accuracy in storage, retention, and retrieval, memory requires the skillful exercise of "narrative imagination" through selective judgment and meaningful participation in decisions about what and how to remember, as well as what and how to forget.[10]

We agree that concerns over the digital dark side are well-founded. Although memory outboarding occurred long before the silicon chip—e.g., pencil and paper, printing press, tape recorder, and so on—the silicon chip's effect on our brains appears to be more aggressive and comprehensive than that of most previous technologies. We are wise therefore not to underreact.

Yet as much as we share in critics' concerns, we also recognize the Internet's potential to strengthen our mental muscles by increasing our speed of information processing and visual attention, and in some cases even reducing the side-effects of aging on our memory over time. There is a growing body of research to support these and other benefits.[11] We are just as wise, therefore, not to overreact.

> Developing technological literacy is the wise response to our digital culture's dark side.

The key take-away amidst all the digital debate is this: developing one's technological literacy is a must since *every* technology, even our most cherished ones, comes with benefits and burdens.

As faithful technological literates, then, it is critical for us to count the costs of the technologies we highly venerate, considering how our gadgets subtly and often without warning or permission shape our minds and impact our relationships with individuals and our environment. In a digital culture, values like infinite storage, maximum efficiency, and immediate consumption of information—not understanding or wisdom or prudence—inhabit our mind's eye and become the measuring stick for how we evaluate ourselves and the world around us. Left unchecked, such values promote a type of *technological idolatry*, or a belief in the power of technology as the path to social progress, personal growth, and happiness.[12]

TECHNOLOGICAL IDOLATRY

"There is something which unites magic and applied science [=technology] while separating both from the 'wisdom' of earlier ages. For the wise men of old the cardinal problem had been how to conform the soul to reality, and the solution had been knowledge, self-discipline, and virtue. For magic and applied science alike the problem is how to subdue reality to the wishes of men: the solution is a technique."[13]

—C. S. Lewis, *The Abolition of Man*

In the next section, we explore the prophet Jeremiah's mental experience of "calling to mind" and how it provides a biblical context for understanding how one's commitment to a growing sacred interiority can promote mindfulness and help lessen some of digital culture's negative effects on our memory.

But This "I Call to Mind"

The prophet Jeremiah, sometimes referred to as the weeping prophet—based on his wish to have a "fountain of tears" with which he might weep for the slain of his own people (Jer. 9:1, NIV)—was clearly depressed, an emotional state that appears to be an occupational hazard for the classical Hebrew prophets. Ministering in Judah in the sixth century and just before the Babylonian destruction of Jerusalem and its Temple, he bemoans, "I have been deprived of peace; I have forgotten what prosperity is. . . . My splendor is gone and all that I had hoped from the Lord. I remember my affliction and my wandering, the bitterness and the gall. I well remember them, and my soul is downcast within me" (Lam. 3:17–20, NIV). So, what does Jeremiah do in his despondency?

Filled with gloom, he suddenly turns his gaze heavenward: "Yet this I call to mind and therefore I have hope" (Lam. 3:21, NIV). What he next calls to mind is very familiar to many since it provides the chorus in the glorious hymn "Great Is Thy Faithfulness." Jeremiah proclaims, "Because of the Lord's great love we are not consumed, for his compassions never fail. They are new every morning; great is your faithfulness" (Lam. 3:22–23, NIV).

THE SOURCE OF YOUR DEPRESSION

"Your depression is connected to your insolence / And your refusal to praise. If a man or woman is / On the path, and refuses to praise—that man or woman / Steals from others every day—in fact is a shoplifter!"[14]

—Rumi, thirteenth-century poet

Jeremiah, in the verses above, is calling to mind from his internal mental bank of stored insights an overarching assertion that shakes his tower walls of isolation and dejection. The mental act of retrieval, as well as the theological truth he retrieves, allows him to be freed from a prison of despair and reexperience the gift of hope, the necessary grace for any journey requiring endurance. Hope is, operationally, the purpose behind persistence.

Hope is like a giant bird swooping down to Jeremiah's valley of despair, grabbing him with its giant claws and flying the prophet to a heightened perch so that he can see the promised land beyond his present circumstances. But unlike William Penn's prison in seventeenth-century England, this perch has no walls or bars. Hope is what ultimately clarifies the "whys" of our life's path and connects them to whatever we may be thinking or feeling, reading or viewing, posting or deleting in any given moment. It is why reestablishing hope is essential for anyone tempted to give up on a difficult but necessary journey. Again, hope is the purpose behind persistence.

HOPE SOARS

"Hope is the thing with feathers– / That perches in the soul– / And sings the tune without the words– / And never stops—at all— . . ."[15]

—Emily Dickinson, American poet

Like Jeremiah, we are naturally in the habit of calling something to mind, and not just when we are depressed.[16] Whether involved in mindless distractions or the details of our favorite weekly program, social media feed, or best-selling novel, we may call to mind that which is fruitful or *sacred*. At other times we may call to mind that which is unfruitful or *profane*, even with our best and most sacred intentions in mind. It is not that our thought life with its habits, cycles, and substance is completely sacred or profane. Rather, it is a complex mixture that is moment by moment either drawing us toward or away from the mind of Christ.

SACRED WITNESS

"Let me be fodder for wild beasts—that is how I can get to God. I am God's wheat and I am being ground by the teeth of wild beasts to make a pure loaf for Christ."[17]

—Saint Ignatius, Bishop of Antioch and Christian martyr (died ca. 108 C.E.)

Our interiority becomes more *sacred* as internal witnesses that are "called to mind" dominate our thought life and engender wisdom, sacrificial love, joy, communal tranquility, and other spiritual fruit. Such is the effect of the words of patriarchs meant to be written in our hearts (see Deut. 4:1–14; Josh. 1:7–9); the words of prophets meant to ignite our passion and confront social injustices (Mic. 6:8); the words of Christ meant to richly indwell us (Col. 3:16); and the dying words of martyrs meant to place our sacrifices in context.

In contrast, our interiority becomes more *profane* as internal witnesses rule our thought life and wreak havoc through worry, envy, fear, lust, and pride. Our worries about what might happen to what we own and what we have achieved have a way of dominating our interiority without our conscious decision. Our envy of someone else's success we would prefer to be ours can likewise dominate. Our lusts have a way of suffocating a variety of healthy pleasures. And our pride subtly jaundices everything with a self-satisfaction that "calls to mind" only self-justifications. Too

INVISIBLE POWERS

"Temples have their sacred images; and we see what influence they have always had over a great part of mankind; but in truth, the ideas and images in men's minds are the invisible powers that constantly govern them; and to these they all pay universally a ready submission."[18]

—Jonathan Edwards, eighteenth-century Protestant theologian

often our heart is filled with the binding effect of divided desires, dulled by continuously competing voices that are not consistently silenced by one champion voice.

In resisting and responding to the temptations and distractions of life, we are hopefully in Jeremiah's habit of calling something sacred or fruitful to mind. Consider Jesus's response to Satan's temptation in the wilderness in Matthew 4:1–22. Each of Satan's three temptations is dismantled by Jesus quoting Scripture from memory. Jesus was too poor to own a private copy of the Torah, and it was not as if he repeatedly rehearsed his response or employed a handy omniscience to foresee the exact angles and strategies of his enemy. His subsequent replies to Satan's intense pressures were drawn from the enormity of a thought life and purpose dominated by his delight in the word of his Father.

The example of the Apostle Peter's sacred interiority at Pentecost (Acts, chapter 2) is also gripping. Like Jesus he did not own a pocket-sized copy of the Hebrew Testament but was able to extemporaneously retrieve sections of Joel 2, Psalm 16, and Psalm 110 from his memory on command to serve the thousands still stunned by the thunderous arrival of the Holy Spirit. Ultimately, his impromptu eight-minute sermon changed the course of church history as three thousand of that original audience cried out, "Sign me up!"

> Sacred interiority is depth. It allows you to stand against the forces of opposition. It shines light into the darkness.

Later, in explaining to the Sanhedrin the healing of the paralytic who was stationed as a beggar at the temple gate called "Beautiful" (Acts 3:1–10), Peter extemporaneously retrieves the lynchpin prophetic verse of the psalmist, "The stone the builders rejected has become the cornerstone" (Ps. 118:22, NIV). When members of the Sanhedrin saw the courage of Peter and fellow disciple, John, realizing that they were unschooled, ordinary fellows, they were astounded (Acts 4:13). Peter, the fisherman, after a three-year apprenticeship with the Messiah, became Peter the teacher and preacher. His formidable sacred interiority provided a stunningly precise framework for understanding the marvelous but unsettling miracle at Pentecost. Out of the abundance of his heart (see also Matt. 12:34) he spoke forth, retrieving the truths from his sacred interiority that redeemed that moment of inquiry.

The Apostle Paul's evangelistic defenses and appeals, whether before an angry mob in Jerusalem or his discourse before Governor Felix, were not read from a book. Neither did he employ notes because in those moments they were unnecessary. His extemporaneous engagements, boldly proclaiming the truth of the gospel regarding righteousness, self-control, and the judgment to come poured forth from a prepared mind (Acts 24:25).

As Jeremiah, Jesus, and the apostles demonstrate, avoiding a life dominated by the shadows and shallows requires our commitment to cultivating a robust sacred interiority. It is a sacred interiority that houses truths, graces, and joys worth dwelling on and worth returning to in moments of temptation, boredom, depression, and even delight.

As it relates to our dance with pop culture, the deeper and broader our sacred interiority, the thinner the distractive temptation. The more we must call things to mind immediately without the aid of our outboard brains, the less needy we are for alternative states of novelty and the less susceptible we are to extended periods of uninterrupted mindlessness. It is our deep interior repository of biblically informed truths and graces developed habitually over time that help us identify in any moment what is wisely ordered and reject that which is foolishly ordered.

Conclusion

Like Jesus and the apostles, Quaker founder and tower prisoner William Penn retrieved truths on command as circumstances invited him to redeem them. In solitary confinement his soul remained nourished by the bread of life, by truths that informed his courage and strengthened his resolve. His was a depth of sacred interiority not easily dislodged from eternal moorings by the distractions provoked by seas of emotional agitation. His highly developed sacred interiority helped him to redeem the time, not merely to kill it.

The development and payoff of sacred interiority will not happen unless we first commit to a program of memorization that faithfully moves God's truths and graces to the tablets of our hearts and to the central hubs of our thinking habits. As is clear in the biblical witness, we human creatures  Sacred interiority helps us to keep track of heaven's priorities. tend to forget what we should remember and remember what we should forget. Without such daily reminders of eternal essentials, we can lose track of heaven's priorities and find ourselves consumed in trivial pursuits. We take up these matters in chapter six as we consider practical ways to build one's sacred interiority through a process we describe as "stewarding the stirrings of the soul."

Let's Get Practical

1. Step One: in your pop culture journal, for one week make a list of five to ten verses, quotes, and stories that have inspired you and are worthy of memorization. They must be truths worth retrieving every day, inviting you to recite them, and meditate upon them.

2. Step Two: then, at the end of the week, put each verse, quote, or story on a separate 3 x 5 note card. (If you prefer to do this electronically, make sure you keep each inspirational item separate rather than in one long list.)

3. Step Three: next, try memorizing just one verse, quote, or story every day. You will discover your memorization pace, whether it should be sped up or slowed down, after a few days of practicing. Be patient. Do not forget that successfully developing any new habit, including the mental work of stewarding the stirrings of your soul, will take time. Each time you memorize something new, it helps to rehearse what you memorized from the day before. Work toward a goal of five to ten verses, quotes, and stories you can enact at one time. Recite these items every other day for two weeks. Then move on to creating another list of five to ten items.

Discussion Questions

1. Is your default mode one of "outboarding" your brain?

2. What are the effects of a lack of sacred interiority on our spiritual growth? Do you think the lack of a vigorous sacred interiority can cause us to forget what we should remember?

3. What challenges do you anticipate when it comes to cultivating your sacred interiority? To developing a robust memorization program?

Chapter 6

Stewarding the Stirrings of the Soul
(The Holy Habit of Remembrance)

"Do not forget my teaching, but keep my commands in your heart, for they will prolong your life many years and bring you peace and prosperity. Let love and faithfulness never leave you; bind them around your neck, write them on the tablet of your heart. Then you will win favor and a good name in the sight of God and man."

—PROVERBS 3:1–4 (NIV)

"And when he had given thanks, he broke it and said, 'This is my body, which is for you; do this in remembrance of me.'"

—1 CORINTHIANS 11:24 (NIV)

SEVERAL YEARS AGO, WE led a retreat for local pastors. About thirty-five women and men were comfortably settled in, away from the demands and pressures of pastoral life. During the first session one of us asked what we thought was a simple question: "When was the last time you were inspired?" By "inspired" we meant when was the last time a light was turned on in a room in your mind that prior to the encounter seemed dark or dull? Or when was the last time you turned a corner in your understanding of an important concept or idea, or what it meant to be joyful?

Given our audience we expected an avalanche of responses. Instead, the room grew strangely quiet, followed by some faint sounds of nervous laughter. We asked, "Is some of the difficulty in responding because you are not prepared to call those encounters to mind from memory on command?" Most agreed. Unless the inspiring verse, quote, story, or encounter happened very recently, most were simply unable to bring the past into the present.

When was the last time you were inspired?

Although moments of inspiration come and go, "having been inspired never passes."[1] If we are able to retrieve an inspirational encounter from the past, then the encounter may become an oasis of the mind ready to help redeem the present moment. We define this process as *stewarding the stirrings of the soul*, or a habitual movement leading toward greater sensitivity of life's inspirational encounters (soul-stirrings) and a commitment not to forget them (stewarding). It includes wise seeking and, once found, wise treasuring of the beauty, truth, and goodness of all of God's gifts.

CONSECRATED AND DEDICATED

"It is a very important consideration that we be consecrated and dedicated to God. It means that we may think, speak, meditate, and do all things only in view of His glory."[2]

—John Calvin, sixteenth-century French theologian
and Protestant Reformer

In conversation with others about stewarding the stirrings of the soul someone inevitably remarks, "Why bother? I can just look it up!" Need to know the name of the fourth bishop of Antioch, the third Roman Emperor, the World Series' champions of the last forty years? No problem. The answer online is provided quicker than the time it takes you to look it up in the encyclopedias on the bookshelves upstairs. (Oh, that's right, you do not have those, and if you did you or your parents gave them away thirty years ago!) We no longer need to memorize a cell phone number; we can simply look it up. And why not? With the incredible accessibility and speed of smartphone apps, information including inspiring quotes, stirring references, and motivational stories can be retrieved in a matter of minutes, often seconds.

WHAT WE REMEMBER MOST

"We live in the stories we remember most."[3]

—Keith Anderson, *A Spirituality of Listening: Living What We Hear*

But here is the problem in our experience and maybe in yours: more often than not the perfect memory of Silicon Valley fails us, coming two hours or two minutes too late. In those circumstances where we immediately need to retrieve a redeeming truth, contextualizing grace, or clarifying fact in response to a pop culture encounter—or any encounter for that matter—many of us come up empty. We may promise to return to the moment but we rarely do.

When we are not content to remain fixated in our envies, lusts, and worries, the most immediately accessible escape is the 24/7 availability of our mediated pop culture dance partners. This again gets at the heart of why our dance with pop culture is so central to our spiritual formation. For many of us, pop culture engagement is a dominant default mode when we experience mental and emotional agitation. The dilemma of our pop culture saturation is not just its accessibility and the increasing narrative effectiveness of its programming to ensure more scintillating dances and mesmerizing dance partners, but rather, and more importantly, our lack of a balancing, robust, and sacred interior life. Pop culture, inevitably, becomes for many the primary escape route when the pantry shelves of sacred interiority are barren of sustenance. So how do we restock our pantry with the "bread of life"?

Has Silicon Valley's "perfect memory" ever let you down?

Cultivating an Appetite for Inspiration

Stewarding the stirrings of one's soul begins with an openness to the possibility of being inspired by something spoken, something read, whether in the Bible or other sources, or something experienced live in person or through our digital devices. It could be an old truth or nugget of wisdom you once knew but forgot or neglected, or an awakening to something never experienced before. Whenever and wherever it occurs, the inspirational stimulus should, for the Christian, ultimately find its authoritative grounding in biblical truth.

In its most basic form, being inspired comes from a willingness to allow your thinking to be changed, your convictions to be deepened, and your perspective to be transformed. Cultivating a willingness to be inspired is a conscious decision to have your mental antennae in position to be more sensitive, energized, mindful, and committed to stewarding the stirrings of your soul.

HOW TO NURTURE INSPIRATION

- Seek out stories of faithful, courageous, hopeful, and virtuous people.
- Meditate, pray.
- Make a list of things you are grateful for in life and recite it daily.
- Spend time in nature.
- Visit a museum, a nursing home, or a pediatric care facility.
- Research your family tree.
- Read a harsh rejection letter.[4]

We can restock our too-often bare pantry by committing soul-stirrings to memory. The big idea here worth restating is that stewarding inspirational encounters requires a decision to live actively with the acknowledgment that there are certain truths that lend themselves to wise, loving, and authentic living in every moment—insights worth memorizing, worth retrieving regularly, and warranting meditation.

Paul's encouragement to the church at Colossae to "Let the message of Christ dwell among you" (Col. 3:16, NIV) resonates deeply, not as a mere suggestion but as a command to deepen mental retrieval regarding the wisdom of Jesus. For disciples of Jesus, Christ's words are the central reference point around which other insights, truths, and awakenings orbit.

TRUTHS FROM CHRIST TO MEMORIZE

1. "It is written: 'Man shall not live on bread alone, but on every word that comes from the mouth of God.'"—Matthew 4:4 (NIV)

2. "But I tell you, love your enemies and pray for those who persecute you."—Matthew 5:44 (NIV)

3. "Be merciful, just as your Father is merciful."—Luke 6:36 (NIV)

The founder of Free Methodism, Benjamin Titus Roberts, began memorizing biblical passages as a boy in the 1830s. Each week in Sunday school a portion of the lesson plans were devoted to hearing the children perform their recitations. Over a short period of weeks Roberts memorized the book of James. He later stated that memorization was a great habit for "building the mind."[5]

Church history is replete with individuals whose courage, spiritual devotion, and interpretive reflection on the original deposit of faith in Scripture had significant impact on the people of their day and the direction of the church for generations that followed. Works by such spiritual giants as Athanasius (*On the Incarnation*), Augustine (*Confessions*), Bernard of Clairvaux (*The Steps of Humility*), Teresa of Ávila (*Concepts of Love*), or Thomas à Kempis (*The Imitation of Christ*) offer much for us to dwell upon.

 THE ESSENTIALS OF SCRIPTURE

"God has ordered matters so that a Christian who might not be able to read the Bible should still learn the Ten Commandments, the Apostles Creed, and the Lord's Prayer. The essentials of Scripture and everything else a Christian needs to know are summed up in these three. They are written so briefly and clearly that no one has an excuse. No one should complain that it's too much or too difficult."[6]

—Martin Luther, sixteenth-century German theologian and Protestant Reformer

At other times more contemporary works provide material worth dwelling upon. In your authors' own devotional lives, we are frequently inspired to memorize lines from popular songs, poems, or movies. One of our favorite lines is from J. R. R. Tolkien's *Fellowship of the Ring* when Frodo laments about the burdens he faces: "I wish it need not have happened in my time," to which Gandalf poignantly replies, "So do I, and so do all who live to see such times. But that is not for them to decide. All we have to decide is what to do with the time that is given us."[7] Gandalf's admonition rings with gravitas, reminding us of our responsibility as caretakers of creation and God's divine sovereignty over all things. Encounters like these are profound rhetorical bombshells that echo deeply in our interior chambers.

Adopting a Daily Central Confession

In addition to being willing to cultivate an appetite for inspiration and learning and learning to dwell on words of wisdom, one's sacred interiority can be deepened through the adoption of a daily central confession. This central confession best serves our memories, our conscience, and our analytical thinking when, like the Jewish practice of *shema*, it is repeated aloud at least daily. It then becomes fastened like a cognitive resting place, a foundation stone of the mind, a place to lower our inquiring and novelty-seeking anchor. And the "fastening" is an act of litany, an act of worship performed daily. It can be said aloud passionately every day as a reminder of one's ultimate purpose. This kind of daily central confession, or Christian *shema*, is an asserted and reasserted truth that ties the confessor to the Creator of the universe, her responsibilities and privileges within the creation, and the purpose-drenched context of all thought, attitude, and behavior.

A *shema* is a daily, central confession, that reminds us of our ultimate purpose.

The *shema* is the portion of Hebrew Scripture deemed central to Jewish belief and found, for instance, in Deuteronomy 6:4–9. The first three words, "Hear, O Israel," are repeated throughout Deuteronomy and emphasize different central truths and commands, but it is this section in Deuteronomy chapter 6 that serves as the initial and central confession in the Jewish Prayer book. In the Jewish tradition, to recite the *shema* twice each day is to perform a *mitzvoth*, or a sacred duty before God.

AN OLD TESTAMENT *SHEMA*

"Hear, O Israel: The Lord our God, the Lord is one. Love the Lord your God with all your heart and with all your soul and with all your strength. These commandments that I give you today are to be on your hearts. Impress them on your children. Talk about them when you sit at home and when you walk along the road, when you lie down and when you get up. Tie them as symbols on your hands and bind them on your foreheads. Write them on the doorframes of your houses and on your gates."—Deuteronomy 6:4–9 (NIV)

What truths are so central and clarifying in our dance with pop culture that they are worthy of being memorized and asserted explicitly every day?

For starters, one's list might include the Apostle Paul's imperative to the Colossians: "And whatever you do, whether in word or deed, do it all in the name of the Lord Jesus" (3:17, NIV), which is a fitting admonition regarding the comprehensiveness of each moment's spiritual significance. Similarly, Paul's assertion in 1 Corinthians 6:12, NIV ("I have the right to do anything, but not everything is beneficial") is an ethical assertion not only concerning the dietary laws at the center of a Corinthian controversy 2000 years ago but also can be applied today to the contemporary believer's pop culture dance. To this we might add relevant truths found in 2 Corinthians 10:5 and Philippians 4:8–10, to name a few.

And Jesus himself offers a description of the power of visual exposure in Matthew 6:22–23, a truth that can be a regular *shema*-like assertion in our dance with pop culture: "The eye is the lamp of the body. If your eyes are healthy, your whole body will be full of light. But if your eyes are unhealthy, your whole body will be full of darkness. If then the light within you is darkness, how great is that darkness!" (NIV).

Jesus's warning should both inspire as well as haunt us in discerning what is at stake in our mass-mediated choices.

A POP CULTURE *SHEMA*

Heavenly Father, thank you for the gift of media and technology. All good things come from you. Help me this day to discern between what is permissible and beneficial. Help me to develop a gracious bias toward whatever is true, noble, and admirable, which confirms your Kingdom or challenges the powers that be. Help me to remember that in all my pop culture choices I remain accountable to You, from what I watch to what I post. Help me to remember that the lamp of my body is the eye, and that I should make every thought captive in obedience to You.—see 2 Corinthians 10:5

The more comprehensive the truth as it relates to the holiness of time and space, the more effective it will be as a central and clarifying truth. Overarching truths like those listed above can help clarify and situate even the most seemingly insignificant pop culture moments, like switching channels or updating one's social media status. They are compelling reminders that "with God there is nothing without purpose or due signification."[8]

Enacting Remembrance

Finally, building sacred interiority through stewarding the stirrings of one's soul requires a commitment to enact regularly those central truths and graces "stored up within you." Just what might the indwelling of the words of Christ, or the words of the apostles, the patriarchs, or other sources of inspiration look like in practice?

THE LAW OF THE MIND

"It is the law of the mind that that which is not expressed dies."[9]

—E. Stanley Jones, Methodist missionary and theologian

For many, soul-stirrings can be enacted in the middle of massive gatherings when we are prone to feel dwarfed by the enormity of human spectacle. So, while reflecting on your angst about being one face in a sea of thousands at a football game or music concert, you quietly recite Matthew 28:20: "And surely I am with you always, to the very end of the age" (NIV). Maybe you speak out loud 1 John 4:4: "Greater is he who is in you than he who is in the world" (NASB). Or as feelings of inferiority and anonymity wash over you in a sea of messaging, 1 Peter 2:9 may be called to mind: "But you are a chosen people, a royal priesthood, a holy nation, God's special possession" (NIV).

Other soul-stirrings can be triggered in smaller crowds and often during the more mundane moments of life. Waiting in the grocery store line, being distracted by the variety of headlines from gossip magazines that scream for attention (e.g., "Is Celebrity X's Dress Too Tight?" or "Will Celebrity Y Hook Up with Celebrity Z?"), you may call to mind the words of the prophets, ancient or contemporary, or the Apostle Paul's encouragement in Colossians 3:2 to "set your minds on things above, not on earthly things" (NIV). Perhaps you choose to recite Proverbs 17:24: "A discerning person keeps wisdom in view, but a fool's eyes wander to the ends of the earth" (NIV).

Or as a crowd of one driving in your car, you may choose not to be distracted by the randomness of talk-show rants or the wide variety of musical options that easily dictate your mood. Instead, you choose the solitude of reaffirming soul-stirrings and recite the Beatitudes of Matthew 5:1–8 as a reminder of what Jesus describes as characteristics of human flourishing.

Or alone in your room seeking to escape the temptation of another weekend of marathon movie consumption, you call to mind the words of Solomon: "Death and destruction are never satisfied, and neither are human eyes" (Prov. 27:20, NIV).

ENACTING SACRED INTERIORITY

1. What is this pop culture artifact or technology suggesting is the nature of reality?

2. What is this pop culture artifact or technology suggesting about what it means to be a human being?

3. What is this pop culture artifact or technology suggesting about the obstacles to human flourishing and the solutions to help overcome the obstacles?

These and other clarifying words of insight and contextualizing wisdom are sometimes enacted immediately in response to a visual or mental stimulus. At other times, the opportunity to retrieve soul-stirrings from our sacred interiority must, by necessity, wait until the pop culture encounter is finished. Stories well told rarely allow us to be absorbed in the art and at the same time find emotional and intellectual equilibrium from the soul-stirrings retrieved. Regardless of the response mode, practicing sacred interiority allows one to reassert the belief that all of life's events, no matter how mundane or novel, find their ultimate meaning in God.

Practicing Remembrance in the Age of Google

Before you embark on your program of inspired memorization, and before we conclude this chapter, we want to close with a few words of encouragement.

Cultivating sacred interiority and the habit of remembrance at any time and under the best of circumstances is a challenging hill to climb. But in our digital culture, it seems more like a mountain than a hill. The digital culture in which we are all deeply immersed is one that denies the value of *tradition*—which is the repository of important things worth remembering and passing down to generations for the purpose of making us wise and virtuous people. When viewed this way, tradition involves personal responsibility. Community members are responsible for seriously engaging what is passed down, for interpreting it, applying it to the present moment, and preserving it for the next generation.

THE MEANING OF TRADITION

Tradition is the "accumulated wisdom and the resulting disciplines, customs, and beliefs that a people carries from person to person through generational time—all of it nurtured as a living dialogue that includes the remembered 'voices' of the past."[10]

—Quentin J. Schultze, *Habits of the High Tech Heart: Living Virtuously in the Information Age*

In *Technopoly: The Surrender of Culture to Technology* (1992), communication theorist and cultural critic Neil Postman lamented that technological society's most insidious accomplishment was to convince people that the future does not need any connection to the past.[11] Our digital culture's religion of technological optimism championed by the churches of Google and Facebook says that all we need to solve any problem and promote progress is a little more information. More bandwidth. The latest app. Google's mission, for example, is "to organize the world's information and make it universally accessible and useful."[12] Such statements harbor an implicit assumption that the accumulation of information is tantamount to the cultivation of wisdom, as if the solution to any problem presented only requires the gathering of more information.

> Digital culture's official religion is one of "technological optimism."

Such optimism represents "the growing notion that one company—Google—could or would solve some of the greatest and most complex human problems simply by applying the principles of engineering."[13] Google's mission encapsulates the religion of "informationism," that is, a "faith in the collection and dissemination of information as a route to social progress and personal happiness."[14] This "theology" falsely equates information with wisdom, promotes individuality over community, and cuts off people from the past. Such memories, after all, have the potential to dilute one's devotion to the belief that progress and innovation are always the best ways to solve our greatest problems. The past only reminds us of how far we have yet to come. Focusing on the past, then, is a technological inefficiency. It simply does not compute.

Information and knowledge are certainly related but they are not sufficient criteria for wisdom. Wisdom is an elevated level of knowledge that involves a capacity for understanding and using information in ways that benefit one's self and serves others. Wisdom is never selfish or self-centered. It catalyzes the common good. It recognizes the things that are inherently good and right, and what is worth remembering, and how to use those things in wise ways. Wisdom helps us to answers questions like: What is worth remembering at all? How do we pursue happiness as a community, a nation, a species? In answering such questions, information is crucial, to be sure, but its contribution to the common good depends on the presence and exercise of prudence. And remembering is different from learning to locate stored information somewhere on the Internet. The former requires wisdom, the latter technical skill in advanced search methods. Storage is not the same as memory.

Christian tradition recognizes that what is at stake in the act of remembrance is embracing the past so we can faithfully navigate the future. The church is a nurturing community that provides a context for education and growth. Christians believe that God speaks to and through individuals and the church throughout history. Many of the communication problems and crises they faced are ones we currently face. Their courage and devotion to interpretive reflection on the original deposit of faith in Scripture are sources of encouragement and instruction for living well and communicating wisely. Memorization of Scripture and other tradition voices, then, is one way to identify communication wisdom that enriches our lives in practical ways and expands our conversational opportunities with those around us. Tradition offers a pathway to meaning, theoretical unity, and communication wisdom in the midst of our digital deluge.

A community rooted in energizing memories and summoned by radical hopes is a curiosity and a threat to the Church of Google's theology of memory. The practices described in this chapter represent a step toward a renewed sense of agency as digital citizens and faithful Christians. They help to recognize the hole in our heart, to remember what matters, and to get on with the project of

> Christian tradition celebrates the Holy Habit of Remembrance. It stewards wisdom of the past so we can faithfully navigate the future.

wisdom and flourishing for all. Memory cements tradition in our minds, hearts, and daily practices in ways that subvert informationism.

In brief, as you commit yourself to a program of memorization you continue your role as a resistance fighter by challenging the dominant forces of our digital culture while simultaneously helping others imagine alternative, hope-filled ways of thinking and being. By taking part in Web 2.0 worldview guerilla warfare you help yourself—and others—cultivate an "alternative consciousness" that subverts the dominant techno-consciousness of our age.[15]

> Christians are called to be "resistance fighters" who help to create an "alternative consciousness."

It further confuses the technical wizardry of mass data storage with the importance of memory, persistently pushing us to outboard our brains and avoid the time it takes to store truth deep in our hearts and minds. Awareness of how such forces subtly work against sacred interiority may provide the added strength needed in your journey toward the summit.

Conclusion

At the end of our retreat, I wish we could say that the pastors took turns reciting their daily pop culture *shemas*. But the development of a central confession would take time. They did, however, leave our time together encouraged and energized, soul-stirrings in hand and with plans to develop their own programs of memorization. Subsequent retreats allowed us to witness their *shemas* and hear the words of wisdom they each managed to pack into just a few short sentences. Glorious.

As the pastors reminded us, like other "holy habits" such as prayer or meditation, mindful pop culture interaction guided by *sacred intentionality* (chapters 3 and 4) and *sacred interiority* (chapters 5 and 6) can deepen one's faith and promote faithfulness, wisdom, and virtue in our communication with God, self, and others.[16] They can help to cultivate the heart-and-mind habit of alertness to the presence, power, and provision of God in every moment.

In theory, we can "recall" everything with the touch of a button, but that is precisely why we cannot afford to outsource the process of memory formation. We need to be more, not less, involved in the formation of memory, understood properly as a process of contextual judgment. By relying on digital sources, we are not really outsourcing memory. Instead, we are postponing and outsourcing judgment, for instance, to memory algorithms.

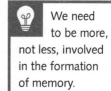

We need to be more, not less, involved in the formation of memory.

In our next two chapters (7 and 8) we argue that in addition to a deepening sense of sacred intentionality and sacred interiority, reframing our dance with pop culture requires a strengthened sense of our *sacred identity*. We offer sacred identity as a foundational portion of our "sense of self," a holy identity rooted in the realities of belonging and separated from the demands of a performance hierarchy. Together, the *Three Sacreds* can help us mentally submit our pop culture desires to God's reality and avoid divided affections that drain energy, purpose, and identity.

Let's Get Practical

1. For one week, focus specifically on constructing a *shema* for your life in general. Like the *shema* found in Deuteronomy 6:4–9, it should be an asserted truth that informs all categories of life, including your dance with pop culture. We shared our own pop culture *shema* with you in this chapter that you may choose to adapt. Start small at first, one sentence at a time, and work your way up to a paragraph.

2. If your church or work has a "mission statement," consider memorizing it. Mission statements are not effective in informing our daily activities unless the they jump off the page and into your memory for easy retrieval.

3. Write your own personal mission statement for your life and calling. Memorize it.

4. Find something you want to memorize and set it to your favorite tune, replacing the words of the song with the verses or quote that you want to memorize. If you are able, write your own song using Scripture or something else you identify as worth remembering.

Discussion Questions

1. Albert Einstein quipped, "Never memorize something that you can look up." How would you respond?

2. Martin Luther emphasized three things that every Christian should know—the Ten Commandments, the Lord's Prayer, and the Apostles' Creed. What would you add to these three?

3. Do you have a favorite line or scene from a movie, television program, song, or novel? What is it about that line or scene that grabs your attention? Inspires you? Resonates with your soul? What does this line or scene teach you about what inspires you?

SACRED IDENTITY

Chapter 7

Dancing with Sacred Identity
(Celebrating Community)

"I praise you because I am fearfully and wonderfully made; your works are wonderful, I know that full well."

—PSALM 139:14 (NIV)

"The Lord your God is with you, the Mighty Warrior who saves. He will take great delight in you; in his love he will no longer rebuke you, but will rejoice over you with singing."

—ZEPHANIAH 3:17 (NIV)

ULTIMATE FIGHTING CHAMPION (UFC), model, and action-adventure film star Ronda Rousey told a popular talk show host that she contemplated suicide in the immediate aftermath of her first mixed martial arts career loss at UFC 193. As the former champ tearfully explained, "I was in the medical room and I was down in the corner, and I was like, 'What am I anymore if I'm not this?' I was literally sitting there and thinking about killing myself, and that exact second I'm like, 'I'm nothing. What do I do anymore?' and 'No one gives a s--t about me anymore without this.'"[1]

You may never contemplate suicide like Rousey, but almost everyone has suffered or is suffering from having an *external locus of identity*, or a sense of

> An external locus of identity is a sense of self-worth based on external, not internal, factors.

self-worth based on external factors such as physical attractiveness, accomplishments, career, possessions, or popularity. You may think of yourself as the successful business person, popular friend, or UFC champ, but such attributions fall short of delivering long-lasting contentment.

In Part One (chapter 7), we suggest that an external locus of self-identity is promoted through two primary mechanisms:

- First, media's glorification of celebrity-seeking supported by the ritualistic promotion of social hierarchies; and

- Second, technology that fosters a "collaborative self" based primarily on the digitally constructed perceptions and approvals of others.[2] Over time such forces can dominate one's sense of self and interfere with the development of *sacred identity*, or a holy sense of self rooted in the twin realities of belonging and acceptance of the biblical declaration that we are made in the image of God.

Then, in Part Two (chapter 8), we explore two strategies to help cultivate sacred identity and transcend the damaging realities of celebritysm and social media self-aggrandizement. First is the biblical wisdom of being "no respecter of persons," and second is Francis de Sales's "Old Lesson" on the importance of sowing our desires in our own garden.[3] We suggest that these strategies can help liberate us from the dictates of unrelenting social hierarchies in our everyday lives.

Social Hierarchies and Pop Culture Celebritysm

A social hierarchy is a ranking of people in which each level is subordinate to the ranking above it. Hierarchies are like rungs on a ladder. Those higher on the ladder are usually more well-known for their achievements, positions, or personalities or have more prestige than those on lower rungs of the ladder.

> A social hierarchy ranks you above or below others. You are a celebrity to those below you. We live in multiple hierarchies.

All of us reside somewhere along a ladder of celebrated—or "celebrity"—significance in the social hierarchies to which we belong. At home we refer to the "favorite son" and the "black sheep" of the family. At work we use phrases like "golden child," "rock star," or "low man on the totem pole." Some are best friends while others are merely acquaintances. Rightly or wrongly, ladders of affection or prominence strongly influence our self-worth. The difficult reality is that many of us are dissatisfied with our current place in any number of social hierarchies.

 ## CLIMBING THE LADDER

"It seems only natural that people should want to climb back up . . . the 'ladder of renown,' yet this is natural only in a society where celebrity suggests economic and symbolic empowerment and anonymity suggests economic and symbolic disempowerment."[4]

—Su Holmes, *Framing Celebrity*

Such hierarchies have several defining characteristics. First, each is governed by ruling *high priests* at the top rung who ensure confirmation of and submission to the existing order.[5] Parents in families and bosses in workplaces make sure we understand why they are higher up the ladder. In groups of friends if you defy the unstated rules confirming the social dynamic of the hierarchy, then you will be put in your place.

Second, these ruling high priests are *guilt-inducing* and work hard to preserve the very symbols that place them prominently at the top. So the middle-aged associate professor struggling for tenure after failed attempts at publication is shamed by the younger, rising academic star whose publication graces the cover of the field's dominant journal (the significant journal publication being a symbol of power within an academic hierarchy). The young pastor of the struggling country church knows her status at the denomination's national convention by comparing achievements and congregational size with friends from seminary. The new plumbing apprentice, cursing his repeated error, also knows his place on the bottom rung.

 ## SYMBOL MAKERS

"Man is / the symbol-using (symbol-making, symbol-misusing) animal / inventor of the negative (or moralized by the negative) / separated from his natural condition by instruments of his own making / goaded by the spirit of hierarchy (or moved by the sense of order) / and rotten with perfection."[6]

—Kenneth Burke, *Language as Symbolic Action: Essays on Life, Literature and Method*

Third, our lives are inescapably linked to these types of pecking order realities and the *goading effects* of those who dominate them. An award-winning journalist friend told us about having dinner with other mutually respected writers. The conversation eventually turned to each guest clumsily trying to outdo the status of the other by jockeying for proper placement on the ladder of journalistic significance. They dropped names of politicians interviewed, size of readership, and number of supporting staff. Our friend left the dinner feeling embarrassed by his attempts to outdo his fellow writers.

Feelings of insult, no matter what our age or circumstances, can often be traced to the wounds of being demoted or dismissed from our self-perceived place in a certain social hierarchy. When we are offended or insulted, it often gives us an important insight into who we view ourselves to be. The experience is an invitation to investigate the hierarchical system in which we feel demoted. If we desire to clarify and strengthen our sacred identity, these insights about insults should be stewarded for all the formative potential they offer.

THE IDEAL SELF

"Your image of yourself is always an *ideal*, which must be lived up to. If you cannot live up to it, the result is a crisis, which leads either to a redefinition of yourself or to neurosis, a compulsive self-delusion."[7]

—Richard Hornsby, *The End of Acting: A Radical View*

Pop Culture Celebritysm

Christened "Hollywood," twenty-first-century *celebritysm* is an increasingly influential quasi-religious discourse with three acts—Act One: Anonymous; Act Two: Discovered; Act Three: Ascension—that publicizes "representations of fabulous quality" and the possibility of escaping anonymity.[8] Hollywood comprises the most comprehensive, accessible, and intimidating social hierarchical ladder in contemporary Western-style societies.

Hollywood is more than a city of movie studios and stars that reside in California. Hollywood is best understood as a complex mechanism that produces a most significant commodity of "knownness" by transmitting to the masses self-identity markers such as beauty, wealth, prominence, and success. Through the organized application of pop culture platforms over time, Hollywood elevates an individual or group to the highest possible rung on a global social hierarchy that swallows up all other hierarchies of significance.

Hollywood is a machine that commodifies knownness based on external characteristics like beauty and prominence.

Hollywood's *comprehensiveness* speaks to the notion that everyone is included: from the masses of anonymous peasants on the bottom rungs of the ladder to the first-name recognition royalty at the top. It also refers to the shadow it casts on all lesser and subservient social hierarchies. Even if you reach the top rung of the ladder in your plumber's union or college debate team, for instance, very few of us will ever rise to the heights of global mass or social media knownness.

Furthermore, other ladders of status are simply not comparable to Hollywood in their *inclusivity*. The thirty-five-year-old is no longer subject to the popularity pecking order of high school adolescence. The retiree no longer cares about union rules or corporate promotion. These hierarchies are escapable, but Hollywood's omnipresence is not. Nearly everyone at any time can access information regarding their Hollywood hierarchical status—from celebrity gossip and pop-up ads to the inadvertent gaze of a magazine cover while standing in a checkout line.

The *intimidating* quality of Hollywood's hierarchy refers to its ability to subject observers to the pangs of constant negative comparison between the fabulous "haves" and less fabulous "have-nots." A popular put-down of someone often includes such comparisons: "You may be good, but you will never be the '_____' (fill-in-the-blank with a widely known celebrity) of the college debating world!" A former student of ours wrote on a course evaluation, "Your class was good, but you guys should stop trying to be so funny. You don't have your own television comedy special, after all."

We all sit under Hollywood's umbrella of influence and are constantly bombarded with signs of unknownness.

Moreover, celebrities' high priest roles are "guilt-inducing" because their symbols of beauty, wealth, or prominence that are professionally maintained on red carpet walks and in photo-shopped images are not characteristic of most non-celebrity masses. Meanwhile, the "common man," or individual with lesser knownness, soaked in the stew of Hollywood's hierarchy, is perpetually exposed to *who* he is not and *where* he is not in contrast. Such menacing comparisons can often leave the lesser knowns with hopes of one day escaping their own anonymity and commonness, including the very slim hope of finding a place (even if only on the lowest rung) in Hollywood's hierarchy of knownness.

A NATION OF FANS

"The mass media, with their cult of celebrity and their attempt to surround it with glamour and excitement, have made Americans a nation of fans, moviegoers. The media give substance to and thus intensify narcissistic dreams of fame and glory, encourage the common man to identify himself with the stars and to hate the 'herd,' and make it more and more difficult for him to accept the banality of everyday existence."[9]

—Christopher Lasch, *Culture of Narcissism: American Life in an Age of Diminishing Expectations*

Evidence of this desire to escape the nagging commonness of non-celebrity existence is found in our natural tendency early in life to participate in imagined hierarchical ascension. As adolescents we sing into our hairbrush microphones before thousands of adoring fans and practice our home run trots in the backyard. At some point in life, our self-identity becomes at least partially occupied with dreams of becoming worthy enough to warrant an audience's gaze. Researchers report that in young adulthood most individuals consider life goals related to extrinsic values such as fame, image, and money to be more important than those related to intrinsic values such as self-acceptance, affiliation, and community.[10] Psychologists describe the basic human need to be known and seek the fulfillment of attention and approval from others as the "fame motive" and propose it is something that sticks with us throughout our lifetime.[11] Companies like "Famous For a Day" capitalize on this motive by offering a megastar package for several thousand dollars that includes six paparazzi who follow you and your friends around town for up to two hours, a publicist, a limo, and a bodyguard.[12]

THE FAME MOTIVE

"It ends up being kind of a damaged life if you seek to be famous because you can never get there, really, and you can never get rid of it, and it spoils your days trying."[13]

—Orville Gilbert Brim, *Look at Me!: The Fame Motive from Childhood to Death*

In brief, pop culture fails to hold up a mirror to reflect who we truly are or offer helpful feedback about how to ground self-identity in the reality of belonging in our daily lives or in God's truths. Instead, it manufactures pictures of who it wants us to be—and be like—and what we should believe about ourselves by tapping into our most basic needs to feel attractive, successful, and powerful. But self-identity shaped by such influences only serves its own self-interests in the end. It is a projected sense of self that hampers our search for authentic individuality and community.

Social Networking and the Collaborative Self

A friend of ours decided to get more involved in his children's social media activity. One day his son left his account logged in, so he decided to take a look. In a fit of rage, he changed his son's status to read as follows:

> To Josh's "friends": This is his dad. Josh is not—to use his own words—a "hard a--gangsta" who "rolls fatties wit his boyz." He is a 14-year-old who raises baby chickens, sings tenor in our church choir, and volunteers at the homeless shelter. He's never left our town of 4,000 people without being accompanied by an adult. He is a virgin so he does not "hits it and quits it wit da' b-----s." Oh, and he wet his bed until he was 9, was afraid of the dark until age 12, and cried at the end of *The Little Mermaid*.

Our friend's digital castration of his son, which he later and rightly regretted, highlights the collaborative-self phenomenon in cyberspace and the ways social media accelerate the shift from an internal to external locus of identity.

As Josh demonstrates, the second screen provides an intriguing opportunity to "make yourself a me," or write yourself into the person you want to be or that others in your social world would approve of. At the moment you begin to have a thought or feeling, you can test it out and have it immediately validated by others. Positive responses are then collected, refined, and eventually woven into an other-directed, idealized (not real) self in an effort to curry popularity, status, and, by extension, self-esteem. Once established, you feel compelled to market this collaborative identity through as many social media platforms as possible, further blurring the lines between private person and

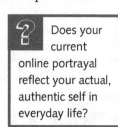
Does your current online portrayal reflect your actual, authentic self in everyday life?

101

public persona. Self-awareness and self-expression ultimately give way to impression management and self-promotion. "Know thyself" in the social media universe is replaced with "show and maintain thyself."

I AM, ONLINE

- *cogito ergo sum* ("I think; therefore I am")—René Descartes
- *emo ergo sum* ("I shop; therefore I am")—Barbara Kruger
- *tweto ergo sum* ("I tweet; therefore I am")—Clifford G. Christians
- *tweto duo ergo sum* ("I am re-tweeted; therefore I am")—Unknown

After learning about the collaborative-self phenomenon, one of our students felt slightly confused. "When others criticize or dislike what I post," she wrote, "it lowers my self-worth. I become ashamed of who I am. But when my messages are liked—even loved—by others, I feel good about myself and like my quirky personality. Am I losing sight of myself? I can feel confident in myself one moment and then disgusted with myself the next. I know this isn't healthy but I'm pretty sure I'm not the only one who feels this way . . . or at least I hope not!!!???"

We agree that social networking provides meaningful and healthy opportunities to satisfy our relational yearnings for connection and intimacy by sharing updates, photographs, videos, and witty quips. But for many, the number of "Likes" and re-tweets received can become quantifiable affirmation of their ascending relational significance in a hierarchy of friends, colleagues, and followers. Better still, your video may just trip the light fantastic and skyrocket you into a notoriety of viral proportions. Exploiting the "Fear of Missing Out" (FOMO), you just might convince someone to dive into

> Have you ever experienced Fear of Missing Out (FOMO)? What drives this fear?

your stream. As your number of positive responses increases, they provide further confirmation that you are not alone in the universe and that your poses and postures, even if pathetically inauthentic like our friend's son, somehow might affect others.[14]

Faced with the promise of hierarchical ascension and the escape from the tedium of everyday life, we rarely stop to consider the consequences of our often-mindless social media immersion. Just as a frog placed in a pot of water does not sense it is going to die if the water is heated slowly, few of us have any notion of the dramatic changes slowly but surely occurring within. In our efforts to garner attention and approval we slowly manipulate our persona, secretly wondering if the real self is truly worthy enough to be liked by anyone or generate more than just a few "Likes."

 Each external identity is a limited interpretation of who we really are or want to be. The sum of our external identities is far less than the whole of our humanness.

Ironically, in shaping our identity to conform to what others find acceptable, we relinquish the very uniqueness we should cherish. When the attributes of our identity are externalized, those external attributes ultimately end up controlling us. As our false persona fails to deliver contentment, we hold on to it even more vigorously because of its promise and power to generate positive self-worth. We fail to recognize that each external identity is a limited interpretation of who we really are or really want to be, and that the sum of our external identities is far less than the whole of our humanness.

In contrast to our culture's emphasis on identity being dominated by various hierarchical orders of prominence, the Bible does not associate our identity with hierarchical realities at all. In Scripture, the dominant emphasis is on belonging. It is "I *belong*; therefore, I am."

Sacred Identity: Invited to God's Wedding Feast

Sacred identity—that is, self-identity that is holy and not deluged and tainted by the culture's system of hierarchical placement and near-constant competitiveness—is first and foremost about *belonging*. Ideally, belonging is the foundational core or hub of our self-identity in several distinct ways.

First, we belong to our family. Like our belonging to God and his human creation, our existence and identity is deeply tied to belonging to a specific family. This sense of belonging is not tied to whether we are favored among our siblings. Our family identity is tied up in belonging to a unit that is separate from the prodding realities of prominence. Sexual expression within marriage, for instance, is an expression of family belonging. The marriage bed is protected and contextualized by covenant and a

 Our value as human beings is tied to our belonging to the human family as God's image bearers (Gen. 1:26–28).

symbolic statement about marital belonging. It is not affiliated with an unending litany of sexual performance comparisons.

Second, we belong to our Creator. Our value is not tied to our placement along a hierarchical ladder of spiritual prestige. Our value as humans is tied to our belonging to the human family as God's image bearers and the unique task for which he has placed us on earth—that is, to cultivate and take care of the garden (Gen. 2:15). This belonging to God is waist-deep in the graces of the past, including the wisdom and folly of our earliest spiritual forbearers and their journey in discovering the necessity of faithful belonging.

Third, the Bible describes believers—most importantly—as belonging to Jesus Christ and his church. Practicing the necessary art of thinking wisely about our self-identity thus requires regular pondering about our belonging to Jesus Christ. This will mean thinking about the clarifying impact on our identity of being crucified with Christ, baptized into his death, and being risen with him. Our identity emphasis should not be dominated by aspirations of rising up the charts of ministerial renown or boosting post views or "Likes." Our belonging to Jesus Christ means we are invited to the ultimate wedding reception—and there is no seating chart.

> A biblical sense of self requires regular reflection about what it means to be crucified with Christ, baptized into his death, and risen with him.

Identity being problematically connected to hierarchical placement seems implicit in various groups of the first-century church. The Apostle Paul tells the Galatian church, "If anyone thinks they are something when they are not, they deceive themselves" (Gal. 6:3, NIV). Paul is warning against self-inflated assessments of hierarchical status. Expending energy to confirm one's status is not only a waste of time, but it also demonstrates a lack of self-awareness and ignorance about the nature of the church as the Body of Christ. Such presumption, to put it mildly, is not humanity at its best and is the antithesis of the gospel of belonging.

The Apostle Paul continues: "Each one should test their own actions. Then they can take pride in themselves alone, without comparing themselves to someone else, for each one should carry their own load" (Gal. 6:4–5, NIV). Hierarchical status, whether in a circle of friends, a community of artists, or a leadership team on a church staff, is often confirmed by an emphasis on comparisons. Among other things, this could mean comparing wit, philosophic insight, and performance in conversation in the field or on stage. Here Paul provides both a *diagnosis* (too many competitive comparisons of talents, gifts, and contributions) and a *prescription* (cultivate the mental habit of self-examination, not confirmation by comparison).

 Comparing our talents and contributions to others results in feelings of spiritual arrogance on the one hand or spiritual inferiority on the other.

The over-concern about hierarchical placement was also evident among Jesus's disciples. It was not just the Pharisees whom Jesus chided for choosing the places of honor at the table in Luke 14:7–11, but also James and John for requesting positions of prominence at their Messiah's right and left hand. In Mark 10:35–45, Jesus essentially told the sons of Zebedee that their hierarchical desires were wasted energies and selfishly ambitious lusts for power and prominence. In Luke's Gospel, Jesus intervened in an argument among the disciples as to which of them would be "the greatest" (9:46–50, NIV).[15] He reminds them that "the greatest among you will be your servant" (Matt. 23:1, NIV).

The emphasis of Jesus Christ and the Apostle Paul is that the habit of comparison as a primary instrument of identity should be minimized. If not, it can plunge us into one of two danger zones. First, if the habit of comparison causes us to feel superior in our heightened status, then we may find ourselves in the blinding spell of arrogance. Second, if comparisons with others are regularly evoking a sense of inferiority, we can find ourselves with a reduced sense of who we are (i.e., our "belonging") and our mission in the world.

How often do you compare yourself to others? What personal needs do such comparisons fulfill?

While belonging to Christ as a daughter or son in his regal family, there is the wilderness journey to travel from baby levels of relational trust to mature adult levels experienced incrementally over time. There is one family; everyone, like Joseph, wears an "ornate robe" (Gen. 37:3, NIV). Everyone is celebrated; everyone is granted graces sufficient to faithfully serve all. Individual identity gets its first and most foundational hints in the fact of belonging, not in our efforts to outperform and outshine others, nor in our ability to rise up the ladder of ministerial, athletic, academic, artistic, or social media prominence.

THE SUPERIOR SELF

"Remember that there is nothing noble in being superior to *some other man*. The true nobility is in being superior to your previous self."[16]

—W. L. Sheldon, philosopher and author

Conclusion

In defeat and lacking a clear sense of sacred identity, former UFC champ Ronda Rousey felt worthless and ready to end her life, overcome by feelings of shame after losing her place on the highest rung of a particular social hierarchy. Her response illustrates the dark side of a sense of self based primarily on one's external roles in society and the perceptions of others.

For all the wonderful, life-enhancing accomplishments of the past two centuries, including communication technologies that place the world at our fingertips, the task of wisely navigating the tidal wave of mediated invitations is often complicated, even if not always significant. This includes the challenge of maintaining a clear picture of our sacred identity regardless of our hierarchical standing. Whether we are known by Hollywood and Wall Street or not, whether we are known by many for our position in a hierarchy or have fallen into the crevices of obscurity, we are known and loved by God. True freedom arises when we learn to embrace the fact that we, first and foremost, belong to God as his wonderful and beautiful creation.

"I praise you because I am fearfully and wonderfully made; your works are wonderful, I know that full well" (Ps. 139:14, NIV).

In our next chapter we explore two especially helpful antidotes to pop culture celebritysm and seeking significance in a social hierarchy wherever it may be found. The first is the biblical idea of God "being no respecter of persons," and the second is Francis de Sales's "Old Lesson."

Let's Get Practical

1. For one week, allow someone else to "have the last word." In other words, allow someone to live with the notion, if just for a time, that they are more right, more knowledgeable, more _____, than you.

2. For one week, try to consciously avoid "posing." Such explicit self-framing is a relatively new phenomenon in human history, brought to the masses with the invention and increasing portability and inexpensiveness of the camera. Be more cognizant of when people in films, photos, magazine covers, and billboards are "posing" for you. Ponder the "effect/affect" of "posing" and being the object of someone else's "pose."

3. Before you take your next selfie, read Craig Detweiler's *Selfies: Searching for the Image of God in a Digital Age* (Brazos Press, 2018). How did this book change your view of selfies? Will you continue to take selfies? If yes, under what conditions?

4. If you have felt insulted by something directed at you, consider including it in your prayers. Ask the Lord to help you understand what your feelings are telling you about your sense of status. Remember that a good percentage of the Psalms are complaints—feel free to complain about the insult in your prayers!

Discussion Questions

1. Proverbs 17:9 asserts that the person who overlooks an insult promotes love. How might overlooking an insult be associated with wisdom and love? Do you agree with the authors that feeling insulted is associated with someone disregarding your own sense of hierarchical status?

2. How is jealousy (the fear of being replaced) and envy (wanting what someone else has) tied to status and hierarchy? Are there times when jealousy and envy are appropriate?

3. Have you ever felt the effects of the Hollywood hierarchy on your sense of worth?

4. Does engagement in social media contribute to your experience of social comparison?

Chapter 8

Recognizing God as "No Respecter of Persons"

(The Holy Habit of Contentment)

"Each one should test their own actions. Then they can take pride in themselves alone, without comparing themselves to someone else, for each one should carry their own load."

—GALATIANS 6:4–5 (NIV)

"But godliness with contentment is great gain."

—1 TIMOTHY 6:6 (NIV)

ONE OF US SPENT five years as a counselor in a Christian school in Detroit in the late 1970s and early 1980s. The most challenging moments were always associated with Valentine's Day and the days just before school dances. Students who did not get a Valentine's Day card or an invite to the dance felt dejected and disrespected. In both cases, these social "outcasts" found a reason to talk to their counselor about a class schedule conflict or college application. The conversation quickly turned to feelings of being unwanted and unloved. Any sense of belonging they desired was crushed by an overwhelming sense of being dismissed by the "elites," the "cool" kids, those higher on the social hierarchy—i.e., the celebrities among them. They clearly knew their place on the hierarchy. It was painful. Things have not changed that much.

As we illustrated in chapter 7, pop culture today provides us with glimpses of such adolescent angst and cultural celebritysm amidst a psychological jungle. Rare is the adolescent—or adult—who does not spend fleeting moments pondering the possibilities of greater social prominence and kicking themselves for stupid things said or not said, done or not done. Those at the bottom of the pecking order often face a daily series of dismissals. Those at the top, typically glistening with perfectly chiseled facial features and body contours, reign as royalty, serving symbolically as the confirmers and celebrators of the pecking order. All of this occurs against a vast backdrop of mass and social mediated cues. There are social "haves" and social "have-nots" no matter which stage in life we are in—and pop culture plays a significant role in defining these groups.

> Most of us ponder the possibility of greater prominence in some social hierarchy to which we belong. Why is that?

The two principles—or gentle antidotes—that we used back then to help our students deal with the challenges presented by social hierarchies are just as effective today, and not just for high schoolers. The first principle is the biblical wisdom of "being no respecter of persons," which offers a biblically informed compass to steer faithfully through the hazards of false humility and selfish ambition. The second is the "old lesson" of Francis de Sales, which keeps us focused on sowing our desires in our own garden. Or, more in keeping with our book's dominant metaphor, it keeps us working on the steps and moves in our dance with the Lord, including our engagement with pop culture. Both principles remind us that we need to die daily to selfish desires and culturally mediated representations of the "good life" as we wrestle with what it means to live a contented life, or a life free from the constant pressures of social prominence.

God as "No Respecter of Persons"

The God of Abraham, Isaac, and Jacob is described in Deuteronomy 10:17 as showing "no partiality" (NIV). This concept can be understood from this verse as "lifting up the face" of someone who bows humbly in greeting.[1] The sovereign's recognition of a subject's presence would come in the gracious act of the king lifting up the bowed head of the subject. Genesis 40:13 describes this action when Joseph interprets the dream of Pharaoh's cupbearer, predicting the cupbearer's favored future.

> God as "no respecter of persons" obliterates Hollywood's hierarchy of significance and our dependence on external characteristics as the source of our self-identity.

"Lifting of the face" is a divine virtue, a practical demonstration of the holiness of God and an invitation to share in his passions and his justice. Yahweh "defends the cause of the fatherless and the widow, and loves the foreigner residing among you, giving them food and clothing" (Deut. 10:18, NIV). God invites human beings to partner with him in his sublime concern for the foreigner. Mere mortals love the "stranger" by "lifting their face" in sensitive recognition of their intrinsic worth as God's image-bearers. Human beings, therefore, are called to care for all citizens of the earth regardless of the categorical differences and despite the hierarchical status that too often seems to justify our disregard.

In this light, the virtue of "lifting of the face" becomes a central element of our sacred identity, a sense of self not dominated by the cues of pop culture celebritysm or other social hierarchies in our daily environment. We practice the assertion that we belong to God as his image bearers (Gen. 1:26–28) and assert the same status to those whose face "we lift." As humans, we are wired to be fully alive when "lifting the face" of others. It is an important role that the Apostle Paul references in his letter to the Ephesians (4:1). Paul urges us to live a life that is worthy of our vocation as "face-lifters."

WE ALL HAVE GODS

"We all have gods, Martin Luther said, it is just a question of which ones. And in American society our gods are celebrities. Religious belief and practice are commonly transferred to the adoration of celebrities. Our culture builds temples to celebrities the way Romans did for divine emperors, ancestors, and household gods. We are a de facto polytheistic society. We engage in the same kind of primitive beliefs as older polytheistic cultures. In celebrity culture, the object is to get as close as possible to the celebrity."[2]

—Chris Hedges, *Empire of Illusion: The End of Literacy and the Triumph of Spectacle*

Holiness is indiscriminate in the giving of grace to enemies as well as friends, to strangers as well as soul mates, to the weak as well as the wise, to the anonymous as well as the celebrity, to peers and colleagues as well as competitors. In Matthew 5:43–48, Jesus indicates that social hierarchy should never dictate whom we love, esteem, or adore. Holiness is humble, non-discriminatory service in and through which personal ambition is tied to extra-personal service.[3]

What or who elicits your "reverential gaze"?

Jesus thus subverts the cult of celebrity and concern over hierarchical status with a devotion to service. In so doing, he challenges the performance sensibilities of everyone in social hierarchical rat races. Jesus asks us to look up to him, on the one hand, and to those who reside on the lowest rung of the social ladder. Never does he encourage humans to look up to those whose talents, escapades, and images dominate the landscape of an illusory hyper-reality and who are the talk of the town.[4]

There is little wisdom in the habit of deferential fawning to those higher in the celebrity hierarchy of knownness—the upward, worshipful gaze that blinds someone to the dignity of all. Sure, one might find the path toward Hollywood or Broadway or the upper regions of Wall Street as an inadvertent by-product of one's vocation, but those places should not elicit the reverential gaze reserved for the New Jerusalem.

Perhaps the most explicit application of the importance of godly impartiality is found in James 2:1–4. Showing favoritism, in this case a nearly comical deference to the wealthy, is an affront to the impartiality of God and to the human dignity of all the parties involved. To the discriminating creator of the seating chart, whom James describes as a self-appointed "judge" with "evil thoughts," his impulse to honor the wealthy man, even if motivated by the desire to help the local synagogue's financial coffers, reveals his ignorance of God's love for all. Overall, the prejudice in favor of the wealthy demonstrates a presumptiveness that is always unbecoming of human beings. To the poor man, his life and worth are idolatrously reduced to the rags that clothe him—rags, incidentally, also clothed the Apostle Paul according to 1 Corinthians 4:11. To the wealthy person, attired in fine clothes and a gold ring, the deferential fawning reconfirms a destructive presumption of his entitlement. Likewise, deference to the celebrated "stars," whether in Hollywood or a local church, only reconfirms a similar entitlement.

Being "no respecter of persons" helps us to deal with the negative effects of celebritysm and social hierarchies.

112

Francis de Sales's "Old Lesson"

Francis de Sales (August 1567–December 28, 1622) was a bishop in Geneva and is honored as a saint in the Roman Catholic Church. He is noted for his deep faith and gentle approach to the religious divisions resulting from the Protestant Reformation. He is also known for his writings on the topic of spiritual direction and spiritual formation, particularly the *Introduction to the Devout Life* and the *Treatise on the Love of God.*

Francis repeatedly called to mind the following spiritual lesson, thus to him it was considered an "old lesson": "Don't sow your desires in someone else's garden; just cultivate your own as best you can; don't long to be other than what you are, but desire to be thoroughly what you are. Direct your thoughts to being very good at that and to bearing the crosses, little or great, that you will find there."[5]

> How often do you sow your desires in someone else's garden?

Many of us live in the day-to-day world of disappointments and unfulfilled aspirations. Sometimes these discouragements are fueled by watching the accomplishments and glamour of mass-mediated stars; other times by witnessing colleagues' and friends' acceptance or hierarchical ascension on some social ladder that we have secretly (and sometimes not so secretly) coveted. In the face of such longings, when it seems we are exiled to a marginalized, unglamorous arena or stage, Francis encourages us to avoid the desire to be *someone* else or be *somewhere* else.

Longing to be someone else or somewhere else is simply a disservice to the power of the present moment you are in. Pressed with the pangs of life in the kingdom of God, which often means picking up more than your share of a mess and less than your share of the praise, we must not covetously desire to exchange our lot for the privilege of walking red carpets or boasting about our number of online followers. Only by accepting and living fully in the worshipping and artistic communities in which we live, with assignments both big and small carried out as unto the Lord, can we bring honor and glory to the Creator to whom we belong and whose handiwork we are. Francis de Sales's "Old Lesson" reminds us to faithfully focus on the arenas God gives us. It requires that even the most humble, other-serving, seemingly ambition-free individuals among us should not allow themselves to feel inferior in the face of others' accomplishments.

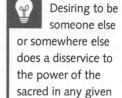

> Desiring to be someone else or somewhere else does a disservice to the power of the sacred in any given moment.

Additionally, Francis de Sales's "Old Lesson" is an antidote to envy and covetousness. His lesson is a reinvitation to take seriously the Apostle Paul's challenge in Galatians 6:4–5 (NIV) that each believer should "test their own actions" or, in Francis's imagery, focus on her own garden, and, subsequently, stop "comparing" herself to others.

Finally, the "Old Lesson" is an aid in our life-long calling to the attitudinal obedience of gratitude. It is difficult to be grateful for the uniqueness of our own life's garden when we are absorbed in envy for the bounty of our mass-mediated neighbor. It is the deepest cause, perhaps, of why our own gardens often remain so deeply unattended and filled with weeds. It is too easy to curse in the middle of the wintry storms affecting our own garden, when balmy tropical breezes remain immediately accessible on our touch screens.

Thankfulness in and for our own garden enables us to invest in what we can have a hand in cultivating, namely, the gifts and graces, the stresses and storms we have been given, as opposed to being enviously absorbed in only what we do not have. Remembering and practicing God as "no respecter of persons" along with Francis de Sales's "Old Lesson" will ground our identities in a sense of belonging to Christ and his family, the church. A sense of belonging, separate from the goading realities of social prominence, is what helps us to experience contentment in our life's journey.

 ENACTING SACRED IDENTITY

1. What are the circumstances in which you feel you most firmly "belong?"
2. What are the circumstances in which you feel most insecure about your identity?
3. Can you identify the last time you felt insulted and explain it in terms of social hierarchy?

Wrestling with Contentment

Despite our best efforts, and even with the help of Francis's "Old Lesson" and other strategies presented in this chapter, finding contentment is easier said than done. The phenomenon of discontentedness is not just true of the twenty-first century. For instance, in the fifth century, committed Christ followers wrestled with the nagging sense of being dwarfed by the accomplishments of others. Saint Augustine's *Confessions* tells of his lust for the acclaim of more renowned oratorical celebrity (that is, those further up the ladder of oratorical fame), a lust that sustained his commitment to oratorical brilliance early in his career. Pecking orders, success ladders, and ambitious mountains to climb are by nature linked to every generation of history and every culture,

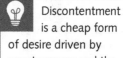 Discontentment is a cheap form of desire driven by covetousness and the impossible pursuit of perfection in all its forms.

shaped by the psychological and physical tensions within each—be it an individual's history, an institution's history, or the history of a continent. In fact, conflicts within religious institutions throughout the ages were not always about doctrine or ritual but sometimes were rooted in hierarchical discontentment. Revolutions galore have been fueled by the rage of negative comparisons between "haves" and "have-nots" in a kingdom's hierarchy.

But past centuries compared to ours did not constantly push announcements about the newly crowned oratorical "celebrities" in our faces, or invite the poor and destitute to compare their sad position in life to the lifestyles of the rich and famous on reality TV at every turn. Nor did they allow one the 24/7 access to social media's multitude of "Likes" sent to someone else, or have an advertising culture that was doggedly committed to their discontentment, hell-bent (literally) on pulling them down to the cheapest versions of desire: the perfect body or job, nicest car, biggest house, hippest clothes, best food, and so on.[6] Unlike centuries of old, we are constantly told that purchasing products will solve our problems, no matter how deep or shallow those problems may be.

 ## THE PROBLEM OF "IF"

"Sometimes I think that all of our struggles with contentment come down to this one word: if. What makes confronting this word difficult is that most of the time we don't care in the slightest about being content. We want to be happy, but in our minds that means desiring things and acquiring them. Yet is all this crying after stuff really a cry of desperation, a cry for help? Maybe we do want contentment but we are afraid of how we might need to change."[7]

—Gregory Spencer, *Awakening the Quieter Virtues*

The dominant framing story for North Americans is one that demands a productive economy, and therefore demands that we turn the consumption and use of products into rituals that ultimately fulfill all our

Consumer desire and religious desire are built on the same basic principle: that material objects *cannot* satisfy human longing.

needs, including spiritual ones. The underlying logic is that everything, including our spirituality, can be turned into commodities for sale. The moment of consumer choice can become so seductive that it may disconnect us from "traditional practices of commitment, such as joining a community or organizing for change."[8] So, instead of joining a community, we believe that reading a book on racism or listening to ethnic music are just as effective as direct involvement. Indeed, books and music can motivate one to action but they should never be a substitute for more direct involvement or engagement.

Consumer desire and religious desire have several important similarities that should not go unnoticed. Both types of desire are built on the same basic principle: that material objects *cannot* satisfy human longing. Religious desire says that nothing apart from God—whether material "stuff," which includes pop culture—or other human beings or ideas can fully satisfy human longing. Consumer desire redirects this principle in a much different way: the endless seeking of personal fulfillment in more and more material stuff. Since material objects can only satisfy temporarily, we need to keep consuming to remain satisfied. Thus, in consumer desire, extended satisfaction is always one purchase away.

The endless seduction of new consumer desire, spread across an unlimited range of available products, can work against the life of spiritual devotion and contentment. Instead of experiencing restlessness as a discomfort or as a reason to change the way we live, we experience it as pleasure. Saint Augustine (AD 354–430) hints at this when he gives the example of someone in a foreign country on a journey home: "They face the danger not only of being so beguiled by the beauties of the foreign land as to forget their goal of returning home, but also of getting caught up in the delights of the journey and the actual traveling."[9]

THE MOST URGENT TASK

"The most urgent task is to destroy the myth that accumulation of wealth and the achievement of comfort are the chief vocations of man."[10]

—Abraham Joshua Heschel, *Moral Grandeur and Spiritual Audacity*

Thomas Aquinas (1225–1274) also spoke of human desire for temporal things: before they are "possessed, they are highly regarded and thought satisfying; but after they are possessed, they are found to be neither so great as thought nor sufficient to satisfy our desires, and so our desires are not satisfied but move on to something else."[11] In other words, we do not regret our restless desires but only their fulfillment. The pleasure typically comes in desiring the things we want, not in possessing them.

To borrow Saint Augustine's language, seduction through material stuff, including pop culture consumption, tempts us to become entangled in the "love of lower things," causing our pursuit of higher things to be "impeded and sometimes even diverted." Rather than turning our hearts toward what can truly fulfill us, we squander our love on the never-ending pursuit of insignificant objects.[12] The sales pitch might go something like this: When lonely, depressed, or bored, then consume. Satisfaction—and contentment—guaranteed.

> Unmoderated pop culture consumption tempts us to become entangled in the "love of lower things."

The writer of Hebrews was deeply concerned about the discontent of his original readers. It was discontent associated with what he called "the love of money" (13:5, NIV), money being the bridge to more possessions, power, and prestige. The remedy to this idolatrous love was a cultivated contentedness with what one already has. The ultimate truth surrounding a deepening contentedness is that God is with us, reasserting the truth originally spoken to Israel in Moses' final days (Deut. 31:6). It is the same truth that must undergird us when stricken by the pangs of discontent over our own garden of gifts, to borrow Francis de Sales's metaphor.

During times of pain or uncertainty, or as we are prone to pursue misplaced desires, asking two basic questions introduced earlier in this book can help bring clarity: (1) who am I resolved to *be* and, subsequently, (2) what am I resolved to *do* in light of my Christian calling? The answer to both questions is wrapped up in the same, foundational, activity: you must practice dying to self, daily.

"The Art of Dying Well"

The idea of denying self, or dying to one's self, as a source of contentment appears through the New Testament and it started us thinking about a spiritual practice that began during a much earlier pandemic time in world history. You may recall from school reading about the Black Plague of the

Middle Ages, which peaked in the fourteenth century, and you may also recall it was the deadliest ever—millions of people died. There were few antibiotics to treat people. It was brutal. And because death was so constant, the church at the time thought that people needed help preparing to meet their Savior and learning to let go of this life and die with grace. They called this spiritual practice "the art of dying well." The Latin phrase they used was *ars morendi* and this spiritual practice was designed to help promote contentment during dark days.

> *ars morendi* is Latin for "the art of dying well" and is a spiritual practice explaining how to "die well," according to Christian principles.

What intrigues us about this discipline is how it applies to more than just getting ready for physical death. It reminds us that no matter how our culture views death, we all have some good dying to do, and on a daily basis. Everybody dies on the way to death—everyone on some level must die to self if they want to grow. So, you have to die to your desire to play video games or binge watch your favorite program if you want to get anything meaningful done today; you have to die to a desire to stuff your face with your favorite junk foods if you want to be healthy; you have to die to your need to control things and outcomes if you are going to encourage others and love you neighbor. And this dying daily is challenging because we live in a culture that tells us that we do not have to give up anything, or die to self, to get whatever we want. We saw a commercial recently for a diet plan that said you could lose weight and eat anything you wanted; no need to exercise either. Really!?

Learning to die well is a form of "good surrender;" it is spiritual submission, a redemptive form of giving in or surrendering. It is not giving up but giving in to what God has willed for you. It is accepting that "this is my life." When we get overwhelmed by our life's circumstances, we can remind ourselves that "this is the situation in which God is instructing me." And then we can ask, "What do I need to die to today that is getting in the way of me being content with my circumstances, whatever they may be?" Good surrender to one's life's circumstances means that one must have a comfortable attitude toward "not knowing."[13] We are more likely to be content when we do not insist that we win or meet our goals in our own timetable, but trust God for what we do not know.

> "Good surrender" is not giving up but giving in to what God has willed for your life.

Good surrender also means that we must learn to change the way we talk about or name our circumstances. A slow download of my favorite program is not a "tragedy" but an opportunity to relax and pray for others. A pandemic is not the "worst thing" that has ever happened in my life (since who knows what tomorrow will bring?), but an opportunity to learn to love God and my neighbor better. There is power in reframing our reality to fit God's plans, and such reframing can lead to greater contentment.[14]

A PRAYER FOR DYING WELL

Heavenly Father, help me to concentrate on being faithful to the task I've been given and surrendering to you in whatever circumstance I may find myself. Help me to learn to die well, daily, to my selfish desires that interfere with being content and drawing close to you. Help me to surrender those pop culture desires that I consume to feel better about myself or to fill a void in my life that I should be filling with You. In Jesus's Name I pray.

To live a discontented life in a contented way requires that we practice *ars morendi* and die to our daily desires, including any pop culture desires we pursue in the hopes of satisfying our deepest heart's needs. As we surrender to the process of cultivating our sacred intentionality, sacred interiority, and sacred identity, we begin to align our hearts with Jesus's heart and begin to see ourselves as God sees us, loves us, and knows us. The "good surrender" is the way to contentment. Thankfully, and thanks be to God, the kingdom of God is not outside us but is within us (Luke 17:21).

Conclusion

Adults can sometimes feel like the forlorn teen, wandering the halls of the high school with no Valentine's Day card or invitation to the prom and no hope of ever making the varsity team. The cards, flowers, and dance invites are symbols that celebrate the high school hierarchical priests, and they are consistently pushed into the faces of the marginalized.

Then we get older and realize that there are different types of proms and parties that we never get invited to, invitations extended to celebrities who will dance in spotlights of prominence while we only watch. And the more we watch, the more our mere spectating becomes a daily sedative to dull the gnawing sense of insignificance.

However, first and foremost, we belong to God. He has provided another audience for the arena that is our life, the "great cloud of witnesses" (Heb. 12:1–5, NIV) watching us run in an eternally significant race.

A "GREAT CLOUD"

"Therefore, since we are surrounded by such a great cloud of witnesses, let us throw off everything that hinders and the sin that so easily entangles. And let us run with perseverance the race marked out for us, fixing our eyes on Jesus, the pioneer and perfecter of faith. For the joy set before him he endured the cross, scorning its shame, and sat down at the right hand of the throne of God."

—Hebrews 12:1–2 (NIV)

Let's Get Practical

1. For one week, try to abandon preoccupation with hierarchical status. Sometimes, especially when we are in new situations where others do not know us and we are trying to figure out our role, we are tempted to be a "walking resumé." Allow people you meet not to figure out immediately how "cool," how smart, how well-connected you really are. When asked what you do, keep it simple. Do not overstate or inflate your position.

2. For one week, consciously overlook an insult directed at you (Prov. 17:9).

3. For one day, listen to music that you know your grandparents would like for at least thirty minutes.

4. In the spirit of Christ's call for us to die to ourselves and our sin, consider a few small things you could die to. Deny yourself one small thing (e.g., dessert, social media, your favorite program, email) every day for a week and then discuss with a friend how this has influenced your contentment.

Discussion Questions

1. Have you been guilty of violating the practice of being "no re-specter of persons"? Have you ever been on the receiving end of such treatment? How did you feel? How did you react?

2. As it relates to Francis de Sales's garden metaphor, how might you be alerted to the possibility of envying someone else's garden at the expense of your own?

3. How is "jealousy" (the fear of being replaced) and "envy" (wanting what someone else has) tied to status and hierarchy? Are there times when jealousy and envy are appropriate?

CONCLUSION

Chapter 9

Conclusion
(Dancing in the Light)

"When Jesus spoke again to the people, he said, 'I am the light of the world. Whoever follows me will never walk in darkness, but will have the light of life.'"

—JOHN 8:12 (NIV)

"And whatever you do, whether in word or deed, do it all in the name of the Lord Jesus, giving thanks to God the Father through him."

—COLOSSIANS 3:17 (NIV)

WE HAVE SUGGESTED THROUGHOUT that the pop culture dance provides for many of us the crucible of our spiritual existence and a significant arena of spiritual formation. Media and technology are wonderful gifts from God to be faithfully stewarded and enjoyed. Yet given their sometimes brilliant, sometimes banal ability to keep us mindlessly swaying on its dance floor, the opportunity to place the dance partner at arm's length and redeem it for Kingdom service seems for many like a nearly impossible proposition.

French mathematician, physicist, inventor, writer and Catholic theologian Blaise Pascal's mighty pen from the seventeenth century warned his readers to ward off the habits that keep us from hearing the

THE SOURCE OF UNHAPPINESS

"I have often said that man's unhappiness arises from one thing alone: that he cannot remain quietly in his room."[1]

—Blaise Pascal, *Pensées*

pounding of our heart.[2] Three hundred years later in the 1960s, Thomas Merton gives a similar clarion call to be free of the "static" of our state of constant distraction.[3]

But we typically love distractions. Too often we ignore our heart's cry for peace and rest. And so the busyness of existence—including nightly appointments with news and entertainment that we somehow have time to fit into our schedule ritualistically—gives us things to do, thoughts to think, and commercials to tolerate. Rarely is our litany of activities in line with who we tell ourselves we are resolved to be and what we are resolved to do. Often it seems there is more resignation than resolution in our existence.

> We love distractions and, in the process, ignore our heart's cry for rest. Why is that?

In closing, we offer several take-aways and reminders from our journey together in the preceding eight chapters. We believe these recommendations are constructive, positive steps toward cultivating sacredness in your intentionality, interiority, and identity.

Several Take-aways

The first take-away is to *monitor your dance*. The ancient wisdom found in Proverbs 14:8 was offered twenty-nine centuries before the beginning of electronic mass communication. It describes the wise as those who "give thought to their ways." A few centuries later the prophet Haggai (at 1:5–7) pleads with his audience to pay careful attention to their own behavioral patterns. Centuries later, the Apostle Paul in 1 Corinthians 6:12 (NIV) asserts that "'I have the right to do anything,' you say—but not everything is beneficial. 'I have the right to do anything'—but I will not be mastered by anything." Paul invites us in all things, including our dance with pop culture, to distinguish between the merely permissible and the truly beneficial.

GIVE THOUGHT TO YOUR WAYS

"Now this is what the Lord Almighty says: 'Give careful thought to your ways. You have planted much, but harvested little. You eat, but never have enough. You drink, but never have your fill. You put on clothes, but are not warm. You earn wages, only to put them in a purse with holes in it.' This is what the Lord Almighty says: 'Give careful thought to your ways.'"

—Haggai 1:5–7 (NIV)

The habit of monitoring—and we recommend keeping a journal of your pop culture activity to understand your patterns—allows us to witness for ourselves the budding possibility of attitudinal and sometimes behavioral enslavement to pop culture that can rob us of daily, restorative Sabbath rest. The biblical admonitions highlighted above especially apply to our pop culture default modes, that is, the time spent with our reward-viewing, relief-viewing, or resignation-viewing (see chapter 2). When faced with nothing better to do, how often are we submerged in the thousands of narratives in our digital streaming carousel? Though it might be slightly frightening or difficult to admit, it is a helpful and healthy realization to discover whether, for instance, resignation-viewing is a twice-per-week or a twice-daily ritual. Monitoring the patterns of our pop culture dance or anything we do regularly can help us understand the core of our desires and how those desires align with our ultimate calling before God.

Reclaiming the redemptive possibilities of life, including the blessedness of play and rest, might begin with the work of "naming" the reason for hitting the dance floor with a pop culture partner during your discretionary time. Such naming, like Adam's naming the animals in Genesis 2:20, is the faithful human work necessary to understand the underlying motivations—whether sacred or profane—that drive our entertainment longings. Naming the context of our longings must include some reflection on the reason for the consumption, whether it be the reward, relief-, or resignation-viewing that we explored in chapter 2.

 Monitoring our pop culture dance helps us understand how our core desires align with our ultimate calling before God.

The second take-away is to *moderate your dance*. If you have discovered that your pop culture dance partner is doing the lion's share of the leading, then you might decide to experiment with pre-arranged ap-pointments with media (see chapter 4). In addition, you might consider cultivating a more balanced engagement with the various dances available with discretionary time. Your options of discretionary time are not just the multitudes of pop culture choices before you but also the freeing opportunities to strengthen ties with friends and family and to deepen your work as caregivers and community servants (also dis-cussed in chapter 4).

> Moderating your pop culture dance promotes a more intentional, balanced approach to your use of discretionary time.

Moderating your pop culture dance may simply include predetermining the time spent pur-suing a certain activity, for instance, limiting your "scrolling time" on a favorite site or app or stop-ping after just one episode of your favorite program. If you are anything like us, thirty minutes can easily turn into three hours. Consider putting your dance on an alarm where the bell sounds after a chosen amount of time. You will begin to discipline yourself after awhile and get restless when you spend too much time engrossed in an activity. The external alarm will soon become an internal one.

Sometimes in discussions with others about their pop culture dance they ask us in a slightly defensive tone, "Well, what is wrong with watching television or surfing the Internet or enjoying three hours of my favorite show as a way to relax?" We do not blurt this out, but when we hear this question, we think we have failed miserably in communicating our central message or they were not listening well. Put another way, it is the wrong question to be asking. In getting into the habit of redeeming our time, the distinction is not always best understood as between consuming or not consuming or between right and wrong but between what is wise or un-wise, or what is of great value or little benefit, given the circumstances.

> Your pop culture dance is one filled with sacred significance and not just a way to pass the time of day when you have nothing better to do.

Moderating our dance helps to assure that our dance partner is not mastering us, and we are practicing faithful stewardship and moderation in all things. Questions we should instead be asking include the ones presented throughout this book, which help us dance with pop culture "in the light," or in ways that are mindfully guided by the overarching responsi-bility to live redemptively, moment by moment, acknowledging the responsibility of wisdom, love, and good deeds. Such questions prompt us to wonder, "Is this pop culture moment the most beneficial way to spend my discretionary time?" How does checking my social media messages multiple times each day help me to love God and serve my neighbors? Does binge-watching my favorite program draw me closer to the sacred or to the profane?

> Monitoring and moderating our pop culture dance assures that we are staying involved in areas where we can still affect the outcome.

The third take-away is to *concentrate more on arenas, stages, and unfolding stories where you can still affect the outcome*. Excessive amounts of time spent spectating others, be it professional sports or drama, can contribute to a passivity that negates the power of the gospel's call to redeem the time. Your marriage, your friendships, parental duties, and neighborhood realities invite you to play a faithful role in an effort to impact the outcome of the story. The lonely shut-in's story is not completed; it awaits the possibility of an intervention from a neighbor or from you. And the presence of authentic community amidst cultural injustices is a provocation to act in an arena and remind others that faithfulness in all of life still matters.

It is important to be reminded of Union Seminary Professor Cornel West's observation that anything beyond moderate doses of spectatorship lends itself to an unhealthy passivity,[4] where we become characteristically unable to engender the sustained energy and commitment to battle in arenas where our exertion can make a real difference. We may be spending so much of our imaginative energies and attention on arenas in which we cannot affect the outcome that we end up making little to no impact on the world in which we live.

The fourth take-away is to *acknowledge that deepening your sacred intentionality, sacred interiority, and sacred identity is part of a lifetime journey*, your life's curriculum, that begins with a commitment to focus on the kinds of questions and practical exercises we offer throughout this book. You do not just wake up one day and decide to be more humble or kind or patient in your communication. It requires practicing humble or kind or patient communication over time in faithful communities

> Deepening the *Three Sacreds* is a lifelong commitment that begins with a commitment to one's ultimate calling in Christ Jesus.

that can hold you accountable. As it relates to sacred interiority and identity, for instance, it includes a daily commitment to assert out loud a central confession, a *shema*, worth reasserting (see chapter 3). Your daily confession reminds you of *who* you are before your Creator (your sense of self; what it means to be human created in God's image); *where* you are in the universe (the nature of reality and how to distinguish truth from falsehood); and *why* you exist (ultimate issues of purpose, calling, and vocation). In the daily whirlwind of distractions, distresses, and competing pop culture voices, such a confession serves as a cognitive hub comprehensive enough to contextualize every encounter and provide a launchpad for faithful action.

ALLEGIANCE PRAYER

"Dear God in heaven, I pledge my allegiance to You. I give you my life, my work and my heart. In turn, give me the grace of obeying Your every direction to the fullest possible extent. Amen."[5]

The fifth take-away is to *develop the habit of understanding your dance with pop culture as an experience that is drenched in meaning*. It bears repeating, as Abraham Joshua Heschel reminds us, that "there is something sacred in every moment."[6] Oftentimes we can get in the habit of experiencing our dance with pop culture as downtime or opportunities to merely veg out and mindlessly decompress. But as we have proposed in this book, your dance with pop culture can be a mindful encounter and an opportunity for serious and joy-filled play and Sabbath rest.

Wise pop culture engagement is to be understood within the biblical framework of Sabbath rest. The refreshment and rejuvenation offered by a story or joke, or alternate narrative landscape, is part of a soulful rest and playful "let's pretend." We are wired to seek rest and refreshment after our work is done for the day. But the responsibilities and privileges of godly refreshment certainly do not include the habit of mindlessly killing time. In the spirit of Sabbath, we should be regularly asking of any pop culture artifact, "What did I just experience?" "Has the experience afforded me the refreshment and rejuvenation consistent with the promise of entering the rest our Creator intended for us?" (see Heb. 12:1)

SABBATH AS RESISTANCE

"When taken seriously . . . Sabbath-keeping is a way of making a statement of peculiar identity amid a larger public identity, of maintaining and enacting a counter-identity that refuses 'mainstream' identity, which itself entails anti-human practice and the worship of anti-human gods. Understood in this way, Sabbath is the bodily act of *testimony* to alternative and *resistance* to pervading values and the assumptions behind those values."[7]

—Walter Brueggemann, *Sabbath as Resistance: Saying No to the Culture of Now*

The biblical record does not appear to encourage the luxury of allowing the image bearer of God to conveniently identify a Sabbath activity, or anything for that matter, as meaningless. Obviously, not every thought or activity is equally significant and meaningful, but nothing is meaningless. The preacher in Ecclesiastes 12:14 closes out his pounding analysis of the nature of existence by jolting his readers with the warning that God will bring "every deed into judgment, including every hidden thing, whether it is good or evil" (NIV). The Apostle Paul in Colossians 3:17 admonishes his readers that whatever they do, "whether in word or deed, do it all in the name of the Lord Jesus, giving thanks to God the Father through him" (NIV). This not only heightens the moral and spiritual responsibilities in our dance with pop culture, it also drenches it with significance in our overarching dance with God.

 THE BLESSINGS OF SOLITUDE

"There are times when solitude is better than society, and silence is wiser than speech. We should be better Christians if we were more alone, waiting upon God, and gathering through meditation on His Word spiritual strength for labour in his service. We ought to *muse upon the things of God, because we thus get the real nutriment out of them.*"[8]

—Charles H. Spurgeon, nineteenth-century English preacher and theologian

Thomas à Kempis, in his fifteenth-century devotional classic, asserts, "Never trust yourself to appear in public unless you love solitude."[9] However, is the twenty-first-century opportunity to sit alone absorbed in social media and pop culture the kind of solitude Thomas is encouraging? Well,

> Does your immersion in pop culture interfere with your ability to cultivate the habit of solitude?

it depends. Reading quietly any artifact—including the Bible—digital or otherwise can be a socially isolating activity. Viewing a film alone that everyone is talking about can with time contribute to a healthy social fabric, or it can thicken the walls that keep us from communing with others.

Just as Victorian critics of novel reading condemned it as a habit of self-isolation, so contemporary critics of social media and pop culture dismiss incessant engagement as, among other ills, something that contributes to unhealthy isolation. What is needed is a wise discerning between healthy solitude and unhealthy isolation. Yes, wisdom again—the key theme articulated a few paragraphs above and emphasized throughout this book. The call to wisdom does not grow stale over time, especially in an information age where "a non-discerning, vacuous faith in the collection and dissemination of information as a route to social progress and personal happiness" is elevated above wisdom and other "disciplined human activities that require time, patience, and perseverance."[10] In this age, a healthy dose of humility and nurturing virtue in authentic communities of faith is more important than ever.

Proverbs describes a discerning person as one who "keeps wisdom in view" (17:24a, NIV). In other words, this is a person who is in the habit of asking themselves (and others), "What is the wisest thing to do?" Not what is pleasurable, not what is easiest, but what is wisest. In contrast, the fool's "eyes wander to the ends of the earth" (17:24b, NIV). The fool is a person who is in the nearly perpetual habit of seeking alternative landscapes, escapist habits that allure him or her with the promises of the new, the more exotic, and more titillating and novel. The fool's eyes—that which gazes and extends longings—keep them in the constant search for the ultimately satiating. But they are gazes and longings generally at the expense of a social contentedness within the family and community in which one belongs.

> Wise use of pop culture is that which moves one away from isolation and toward actualizing an increasingly healthy community.

Social media, as the name suggests, is, ideally, an instrument serving socializing functions. For the Christian, whose social realities are situated in the repeated biblical emphasis on relational and communal fidelity, a wise use of social media is that which moves one toward the experience of an increasingly healthy community.

Concluding our Conclusion

In closing, we appreciate your time and attention throughout the journey of this book. We trust that our promise to deliver biblical wisdom and practical insights has held true for you.

When we *monitor* and *moderate* our dance with pop culture, we find we are disconnected from the meaning and ministry inherent in Sabbath. Too regularly we are engaged in resignation-viewing because we perceive there is nothing else—or "better"—to do. In response, our prayer must be for a broader vision of dance possibilities and the energy to start moving on a variety of dance floors.

Left to our mindless pop culture tendencies, we are like the people Jesus described in his parable about the vineyard workers in Matthew 20—a passage that we introduced briefly as we began our journey together (see chapter 1). Would we press the parable too much to suggest that in a contemporary pop culture setting, those workers standing around the vineyard would not be standing but sitting with their mobile devices scrolling for entertainment options or exchanging messages with friends? We live in a time when pop culture's ability to dominate our energies with a constant array of arresting narratives and seductive services can typically outstrip the relative boredom of our immediate surroundings. So even if we were hired to work in the vineyard, the work would have to be exciting enough to tear us away from our screens.

 Monitoring and moderating our pop culture dance promotes mindfulness that fosters Sabbath rest, love of neighbor, and sacrificial acts of service in our communities.

The underlying and often repeated challenge throughout this book has been to consider what it means to call Jesus Christ the Lord of your pop culture dance—more tellingly, Lord of your bored and listless moments. This is not a gloom and doom challenge born out of anti-technological sentiment. As we suggest, reclaiming the redemptive possibilities of life, including the blessedness of pop culture play and rest and the glorious gifts of story, begins with again asking the question at the beginning of this book: *Who is leading whom in your pop culture dance?* Are you dancing in the dark, led by your default mode of mindless, self-entitled engagement, or are you dancing in the light, driven by who you are and what you are resolved to be as a follower of Jesus Christ?

What does it mean to make Christ the Lord of your pop culture dance?

We hope that our journey together has equipped you to take the lead in your own dance, one step and one day at a time, and to understand how to cultivate mindfully the sacredness of every pop culture encounter. Sabbath rest awaits the resistance fighter who gives thought to her ways and refuses to compartmentalize life's allegiances, ultimate desires, and deepest loves.

To the resistance fighters and Sabbath seekers among us: Fight the good fight. Stay encouraged. Stay grateful. Share your stories. Find rest. Keep in touch. Thanks again for your time.

Let's Get Practical

1. Experiment for a week with the self-examining assertion, "How does wisdom inform and guide my day?" In your journal list at least three pop culture choices each day that you believe were led by wisdom.

2. Make sure to revisit your chosen *shema* (see chapter 6) and practice making it a functional mission statement for your life. Remember that mission statements are essentially dead on the page unless you can retrieve them on command.

3. Review your pop culture journal. Highlight three big ideas you gleaned each week. What do they have in common? How have your daily habits toward pop culture changed in the last month? Last week?

Discussion Questions

1. Is there a take-away from the book's conclusion that is especially important for your dance with pop culture?

2. Is there an entry from your pop culture journal that you would share with a trusted family member or friend? Which one? Why?

3. What might it mean to call Christ Jesus the Lord of your bored moments?

Endnotes

Preface

1. Bob Garfield, "The Persuaders," Frontline, November 9, 2004. https://www.pbs.org/wgbh/pages/frontline/shows/persuaders/etc/script.html, paras. 2 and 21.

An Opening Note to Our Reader

1. Paul Lewis, "'Our Minds Can Be Hijacked': The Tech Insiders Who Fear a Smartphone Dystopia," *OSHO News*, November 7, 2017, para. 7, https://www.theguardian.com/technology/2017/oct/05/smartphone-addiction-silicon-valley-dystopia.

2. We adapt the concept of "resistance thinking" from Christian apologist C. S. Lewis, who introduced the idea in an essay titled "Christian Apologetics," in *God in the Dock: Essays on Theology and Ethics*, ed. Walter Hooper (Grand Rapids: Eerdmans, 1994), 89–103. Lewis suggests the idea of the Christian faith as a "resisting material" and demonstrates how Christians might communicate against modernity and the fiction of progress by practicing an alternative and latent form of argument. This essay and ones on "Bulverism" and "Before We Can Communicate" in the same collection are wonderful introductions to Lewis's ideas on communication. (We would like to thank Terry Lindvall, Virginia Wesleyan University, for his help with this note.)

Chapter 1

1. Blaise Pascal, *Pensées*, trans. A.J. Krailsheimer (Harmondsworth, England: Penguin, 1986), 150.

2. Cornell West, *Prophetic Thought in Postmodern Times* (Monroe: Common Courage, 1993), 6.

3. For all the improved talk about integration of "faith and life" within the Christian community over the last generation, there was little demonstration in our lives that we consciously considered the implications of the Lordship of Christ in our entertainment

impulses and pursuits. Part of the problem was that our entertainment pursuits rarely lasted longer than the time it took to push the power button of the television remote. The arms' length availability of media programming, in most settings little more than seconds away, prevented us from cultivating a self-discovery that comes from the hard work of co-existing with boredom. We will spend more time on the faithful stewarding of bored moments in later chapters.

4. On the "constructive" aspects of boredom, see Stephen J. Vodanovich, S.J., "On the Possible Benefits of Boredom: A Neglected Area in Personality Research," *Psychology and Education: An Interdisciplinary Journal 40*, nos. 3–4 (2003): 28–33.

5. If we were to pick one image that addresses the primary concerns of this book, it would be that of the work-wearied soul, television remote in hand, myopically channel surfing (or searching for videos on YouTube), averaging three seconds per broadcast option through the 150 premium-packaged offerings, and finally settling on one that visually triggers a commitment for at least the next three minutes. And all of it without considering the implications of the Lordship of Christ, or more generally, asking about the moral point of it all.

6. And surprise, surprise, much of it is. We recognize this and want you to know that we agree with many of you that some of it is probably worth bashing, or at the very least, avoiding completely. Finally, for those of you who were initially concerned by this opening salvo, we do think that violence or the gratuitously erotic are not all in the eyes of the beholder.

7. Rod Dreher, *The Benedict Option: A Strategy for Christians in a Post-Christian Nation* (New York: Sentinel, 2017), 2.

8. Andrew M. Greeley, *God in Popular Culture* (Chicago: Thomas More, 1989), 9.

9. See, for example, William D. Romanowski, *Pop Culture Wars: Religion and the Role of Entertainment in American Life* (Downers Grove: InterVarsity, 1996); Craig Detweiler and Barry Taylor, *A Matrix of Meanings: Finding God in Pop Culture* (Grand Rapids: Baker Academic, 2003); William D. Romanowski, *Eyes Wide Open: Looking for God in Popular Culture*, rev. and exp. (Grand Rapids: Brazos, 2007); David Dark, *Everyday Apocalypse: The Sacred Revealed in Radiohead, The Simpsons, and Other Pop Culture Icons* (Grand Rapids: Brazos, 2002); Brian Godawa, *Hollywood Worldviews: Watching Films with Wisdom and Discernment* (Downers Grove: InterVarsity, 2002); Kurt Bruner and Jim Ware, *Finding God in the Lord of the Rings* (Carol Stream: Tyndale House, 2006); Christian Piatt, *"LOST": A Search for Meaning* (St. Louis: Chalice, 2006); John Ankerberg and Dillon Burroughs, *What Can Be Found in "LOST": Insights on God and the Meaning of Life* (Eugene: Harvest House, 2008); and Chris Seay, *The Gospel According to "LOST"* (Nashville: Thomas Nelson, 2009).

10. Robert H. Woods Jr., Kelly Skarritt-Williams, Caleb Chan, Ken Waters, and Divine Agodzo, "Motivations for Reading the *Left Behind* Book Series: A Uses and Gratifications Analysis," *Journal of Media and Religion* 15, no. 2 (2016): 63–77.

11. Annalee Ward, "Themed Destinations, Museums, and Evangelicals," in *Evangelical Christians and Popular Culture: Pop Goes the Gospel*, vol. 3, ed. Robert H. Woods Jr. (Santa Barbara: Praeger, 2013), 244–60.

12. John L. Pauley and Amy King, "Evangelicals' Passion for *The Passion of the Christ*," in *Evangelical Christians and Popular Culture: Pop Goes the Gospel*, vol. 1, ed. Robert H. Woods Jr. (Santa Barbara: Praeger, 2013), 36–51.

13. Romanowski, *Eyes Wide Open*, 16.

14. Barna Research Group, "How Technology Is Changing Millennial Faith," October 15, 2013, https://www.barna.com/research/how-technology-is-changing-millennial-faith/.

15. See Marcel Danesi's *Popular Culture: Introductory Perspectives* (Lanham: Rowman and Littlefield, 2008), 2–5, and John Storey's *Cultural Theory and Popular Culture: An Introduction*, 2nd ed. (New York: Routledge, 2015), 5–16, for clarity on the broader definitions of the term "pop culture."

16. John Dye, "Pope Francis Calls Texts, Internet, Social Media 'Gifts of God,'" *Android Authority*, January 22, 2016, http://www.androidauthority.com/pope-internet-gift-god-669125/.

17. See John M. Culkin, S.J., "A Schoolman's Guide to Marshall McLuhan," *The Saturday Review*, Saturday, March 18, 1967, https://www.unz.com/print/SaturdayRev-1967mar18-00051.

18. This branch of inquiry is referred to as media ecology, which explores how media and technology influence human self-perception and identity, understanding and feeling, and how media influence the way human beings interact with others around them, including their institutions. For more nuanced and precise definitions, see the Media Ecology Association's description, http://www.media-ecology.org/. Media ecology is popularly represented in classic works by scholars such as Marshall McLuhan (*Understanding Media: The Extensions of Man* [New York: McGraw-Hill, 1964]), Walter Ong (*Orality and Literacy: The Technologizing of the Word* [New York: Routledge, 1982]); and Neil Postman (*Technopoly: The Surrender of Culture to Technology* [New York: Vintage, 1992]), to name only a well-known few.

19. Clifford G. Christians, "Evangelical Perspectives on Technology," *Evangelical Christians and Popular Culture*, vol. 1, 323.

20. These helpful questions appear in Bill Strom, *More Than Talk: Communication Studies and the Christian Faith*, 2nd ed. (Dubuque: Kendall/Hunt, 2003), 303. This wonderful book is now in its fifth edition.

21. Kenneth A Myers, *All God's Children and Blue Suede Shoes: Christians and Popular Culture* (Wheaton: Crossway, 1989), 53.

22. See Walter Brueggemann, *Sabbath as Resistance: Saying No to the Culture of Now* (Louisville: Westminster John Knox, 2014).

23. Eugene Peterson, *The Pastor: A Memoir* (New York: HarperCollins, 2012), 270. See also Eugene Peterson, quoted in Andy Crouch, "The Joyful Environmentalists: Eugene Peterson and Peter Harris Think of Creation Care Not as an Onerous Duty but a Natural Response to the Goodness of God," *Christianity Today* 55, no. 6 (2011): 32.

24. Abraham Joshua Heschel, *I Asked for Wonder: A Spiritual Anthology* (New York: Crossway, 1983), 57.

25. Thomas W. Cooper, *Fast Media, Media Fast: How to Clear Your Mind and Invigorate Your Life in an Age of Media Overload* (Boulder: Gaeta, 2011).

26. Abraham Joshua Heschel, *God in Search of Man: A Philosophy of Judaism* (New York: Harper and Row, 1955), 74.

27. Richard J. Foster, *Celebration of Discipline: The Path to Spiritual Growth* (New York: Harper One, 1998), 21. The first printing of this classic Christian book was in 1978; the second printing in 1988.

28. For a discussion of this and other Ignatian theology, see David L. Fleming, S.J., *The Spiritual Exercises of St. Ignatius: A Literal Translation and Contemporary Reading* (St. Louis: St. Louis Institute of Jesuit Sources, 1978).

Chapter 2

1. Neil Postman, *Amusing Ourselves to Death: Public Discourse in the Age of Show Business* (New York: Penguin, 1985), 92–93.

2. We would suggest, from our own experience and that of our students, that an over-percentage of our life unexamined and unaccounted for is made up of the time spent unthinkingly engaged in entertainment options at our fingertips. Easier than rolling out of bed, less physically exerting than clipping our toenails, the vast and varied entertainment options usher us anywhere our eyes care to settle. And the two-dimensional spectacle winning the competition for our visual, then auditory attention for the next three seconds or three hours can bring about a trance-like focus faster and more repeatedly than anything else in world history.

3. Phillippa Lally, Cornelia H. M. van Jaarsveld, Henry W. W. Potts, and Jane Wardle, "How Are Habits Formed: Modelling Habit Formation in the Real World," *European Journal of Social Psychology* 40, no. 6 (2010): 998–1009.

4. For an accessible overview see Susan Weinschenk, "Why We're All Addicted to Texts, Twitter and Google," *Psychology Today*, Sept. 11, 2012, https://www.psychologytoday.com/us/blog/brain-wise/201209/why-were-all-addicted-texts-twitter-and-google; Emily Yoffe, "Seeking: How the Brain Hard-wires Us to Love Google, Twitter, and Texting, and Why That's Dangerous," *Slate*, August 12, 2009, https://slate.com/technology/2009/08/the-powerful-and-mysterious-brain-circuitry-that-makes-us-love-google-twitter-and-texting.html. For a more in-depth, scholarly treatment see Kep Kee Loh and Ryota Kanai, "How Has the Internet Reshaped Human Cognition?" *The Neuroscientist* 22, no. 5 (2016): 506–20.

5. We are thankful to James K. A. Smith's book, *Desiring the Kingdom: Worship, Worldview, and Cultural Formation* (Grand Rapids: Baker Academic, 2009) for this insight on how regular habits shape our deepest desires, the contours of our imagination, and our understanding of our place in the world. See also Smith's subsequent book, *You Are What You Love: The Spiritual Power of Habit* (Grand Rapids: Brazos, 2016).

6. Augustine, *The Confessions of Saint Augustine*, Book X, Chapter 8, trans. Rex Warner (New York: Mentor-Omega, 1963), 219.

7. In Plato's writings from the fourth century BC, "know thyself" is sprinkled throughout Socrates' dialogues. The phrase served as a dominant motivation for conversational courage, and Plato proposed it as a goal in the philosophical dialogues of ancient Athens. Yet the phrase "know thyself" can also be a beneficial clarion call for anyone interested in understanding their dance with pop culture and the various characteristics of their own "trance dance."

8. See Nicola Menzie, "Heartpoints App Helps Christians Track How Well, or Wobbly, They Walk with the Lord," *The Christian Post*, September 2, 2013, https://www.christianpost.com/news/heartpoints-app-helps-christians-track-how-well-or-wobbly-they-walk-with-the-lord.html.

9. Phil Schneider, "Christianity, There's an App for That: Heartpoints Review," *Churchmag*, September 30, 2013, https://churchm.ag/heartpoints-app-review/, paras. 7 and 8.

10. E. Stanley Jones, *Abundant Living* (New York: Abingdon-Cokesbury, 1947), 125.

11. Jennifer Earl, "Dad Creates App That Freezes Your Kids' Phones Until They Answer Your Texts," *CBS News*, August 23, 2017, https://www.cbsnews.com/news/this-dad-created-an-app-that-freezes-your-kids-phones-until-they-answer-your-texts/.

12. For an accessible overview see Caleb Garling, "Snapchat Could Capitalize on Users' Undivided Attention," *SFGATE*, December 11, 2013, http://www.sfgate.com/technology/article/Snapchat-could-capitalize-on-users-undivided-5056295.php. See also Risa Sawaki, Steven J. Luck, and Jane E. Raymond, "How Attention Changes in Response to Incentives," *Journal of Cognitive Neuroscience* 27, no. 11 (2015): 2229–39.

13. For an indepth discussion of *homo narrans*, see Walter R. Fisher, *Human Communication as Narration: Toward a Philosophy of Reason, Value, and Action* (Columbia: University of South Carolina Press, 1989).

14. See Alexander G. Huth, Wendy A. de Heer, Thomas L. Griffiths, Frédéric E. Theunissen, and Jack L. Gallant, "Natural Speech Reveals the Semantic Maps That Tile Human Cerebral Cortex," *Nature: International Journal of Science* 532 (April 2016): 453–58.

15. Abraham Joshua Heschel, *Moral Grandeur and Spiritual Audacity* (New York: Farrar, Straus and Giroux, 1996), 92.

16. Nicholi is paraphrasing well-known Christian apologist and author C. S. Lewis in this quote. See Armand Nicholi, *The Question of God: C. S. Lewis and Sigmund Freud Debate God, Love, Sex, and the Meaning of Life* (New York: Free, 2003), 185.

17. For a thoughtful and scholarly treatment of a Christian perspective of video games see Kevin Schut, *Of Games and God: A Christian Exploration of Video Games* (Grand Rapids: Brazos, 2013).

18. See Ben Spencer, "Mobile Users Can't Leave Their Phone Alone for Six Minutes and Check It Up To 150 Times a Day," *Daily Mail.com*, February 10, 2013, http://www.dailymail.co.uk/news/article-2276752/Mobile-users-leave-phone-minutes-check-150-times-day.html. We recognize that by the time you read this the numbers have probably changed, and we are guessing they are not much different, and probably higher.

19. American Optometric Association, "Survey Reveals Parents Drastically Underestimate the Time Kids Spend on Electronic Devices," *Cision PR Newswire*, July 22, 2014, https://www.prnewswire.com/news-releases/survey-reveals-parents-drastically-underestimate-the-time-kids-spend-on-electronic-devices-268088521.html.

20. We are thankful to colleague and friend Clinton Rothell for this illustration.

21. During the years leading up to the fall of the Soviet Union in 1991, people behind the Iron Curtain assumed film scenes inside Western grocery stores were obvious propaganda ploys of Western capitalists. The Soviet state was increasingly characterized by shortages of foodstuffs and empty shelves. Our movies with acres and acres of food choices, restaurant malls, and the more-than-cornucopia of meats, vegetables, and fruit were beyond their capacity to imagine as anything but fantasy. But we know these grocery settings so well we typically take them for granted. In the same way, people of every past century of world history could not begin to imagine our cornucopia of immediately available pop culture options. To them, the fantasy would both tantalize and terrify.

22. Timothy Keller, *The Prodigal God: Recovering the Heart of the Christian Faith* (New York: Riverhead, 2008), 128–29.

23. The importance of reconsidering our dance with pop culture is rather like the importance of taking another look at our eating habits. Often, we are not pressed to take inventory of our dietary intake until we become aware of a nutritional deficiency or health crisis. Suddenly, especially if the health threat is prominent, we begin to realize that every morsel matters.

24. See Robert T. Putnam, *Bowling Alone: The Collapse and Revival of American Community* (New York: Simon and Schuster, 2001).

25. Richard Rohr, *Everything Belongs: The Gift of Contemplative Prayer* (New York: Crossroad, 2003), 43.

26. David Foster Wallace, *The Pale King* (New York: Back Bay, 2011), 438.

27. Roger Kimball, "What Did Kierkegaard Want?," *New Criterion*, September 2001, http://www.newcriterion.com/articles.cfm/What-did-Kierkegaard-want---2132, para. 12.

28. For an accessible introduction to Kierkegaard's thought see Charles E. Moore, ed., *Provocations: Spiritual Writings of Kierkegaard* (Farmington: Plough, 2002).

29. Andreas Elpidorou, "The Bright Side of Boredom," *Frontiers in Psychology*, November 3, 2014, https://www.frontiersin.org/articles/10.3389/fpsyg.2014.01245/full, para.4.

30. This is an "indifference" which Abraham Joshua Heschel describes as the "root of sin" in his book *God in Search of Man: A Philosophy of Judaism* (New York: Harper and Row, 1955), 43. We are sure by this point in the book you can tell that we deeply respect Heschel's work.

Chapter 3

1. Charles H. Spurgeon, *The Treasury of David*, vol. 2 (Peabody: Hendrickson, 1988), 466-67.

2. C. S. Lewis, *Screwtape Letters* (1942; reprint, New York: HarperCollins, 2001), 34.

3. Susan Spencer, "Driver Says GPS Led Her into Sand Trap in Northbridge," *Telegram.com*, June 20, 2012, https://www.telegram.com/article/20120620/NEWS/106209898.

4. The idea of "intentional living" is a popular catch-phrase that has morphed into a popular self-help movement, spawning scores of how-to books, workshops, and training materials for anyone interested in living a more purpose-filled existence. Described generally as a lifestyle rooted in an individual's or group's conscious attempts to live faithfully according to a set of values and beliefs, it seeks to help individuals live in sync with their God-given design and stop wasting time.

5. John Locke, *An Essay Concerning Human Understanding*, Book 2, 19 (1689; reprint, Greensboro: WLC, 2009), 152.

6. See Bruce Shelley, *Church History in Plain Language*, 2nd ed. (Nashville: Thomas Nelson, 1995), 83.

7. This quote is widely attributed to Dorothy Parker, but it has also been attributed to Ellen Parr. Its earliest appearance occurred in *Reader's Digest* in December 1980 in a "Quotable Quotes" column where the words were ascribed to Parr. We give credit to both women for this great quote. See Dorothy Parker, and Ellen Parr, "The Cure for Boredom Is Curiosity. There Is No Cure for Curiosity," *Quote Investigator*, https://quoteinvestigator.com/2015/11/01/cure/.

8. See Richard J. Foster and James Bryan Smith, eds., *Devotional Classics: Selected Readings for Individuals and Groups* (New York: Harper Collins, 1993), 20.

9. Gregory H. Spencer, *Awakening the Quieter Virtues* (Downers Grove: IVP, 2010), 11.

10. Gordon MacDonald, "God's Calling Plan: So What Exactly Is a Call to Ministry?," *ctpastors*, 2003, http://www.christianitytoday.com/pastors/2003/fall/3.35.html.

11. See Quentin J. Schultze's helpful book, *Here I Am: Now What on Earth Should I Be Doing?* (Grand Rapids: Baker, 2005). Schultze distinguishes between "our shared vocation and each person's particular station." Our vocation is "to be caring followers of

Jesus Christ who faithfully love God, neighbor, and self" (15). Our "stations"—jobs, roles, relationships—are over-archingly informed and contextualized by our vocation.

12. Ibid., 12.

13. See Ecclesiastes 12:13, 14; Matthew 12:34–37; Hebrews 4:13.

14. See Colossians 3:17; 1 Corinthians 10:31.

15. Oswald Chambers, "Shallow and Profound," in *My Utmost for His Highest*," November 22, https://utmost.org/shallow-and-profound/.

16. We contend that "fragmented-life spirituality" is more descriptive and accurate in describing our journey than "divided-life-spirituality." Both phrases describe the effects of a polytheistic approach to life: different categories of life are ordered by different, conflicting ultimate desires.

17. Dorothy Sayers, *Christian Letters to a Post-Christian World: A Collection of Essays* (Grand Rapids: Eerdmans, 1969), 152.

18. Thomas C. Oden, *After Modernity . . . What?* (Grand Rapids: Zondervan, 1992), 31. Hedonism is a philosophical approach stating that the pursuit of pleasure and intrinsic goods are the primary or most important goals of human life. A hedonist strives to maximize net pleasure, but when having finally gained that pleasure, happiness remains stationary.

19. James K. A. Smith, *You Are What You Love: The Spiritual Power of Habit* (Grand Rapids: Brazos, 2016), 88.

20. Abraham Kuyper, "Modernism: A Fata Morgana in the Christian Domain," in *Abraham Kuyper: A Centennial Reader*, ed. James D. Bratt (Grand Rapids: Eerdmans, 1998), 89. This speech was delivered in 1871.

21. Augustine, *The Confessions of Saint Augustine*, Book III, Chapter 3, trans. Rex Warner (New York: Mentor-Omega, 1963), 55.

22. Spencer, *Awakening the Quieter Virtues*, 112.

23. See Robert Schnase's excellent short essay, "The Blessing and Curse of Ambition," *The Christian Ministry* (January/February, 1993): 16–19.

24. J. Oswald Sanders, *Spiritual Leadership*, upd. and exp. (Chicago: Moody, 1994), 14.

25. Oswald Chambers, "The Spiritually Vigorous Saint," in *My Utmost for His Highest*," July 11, https://utmost.org/the-spiritually-vigorous-saint/.

26. Augustine, *Confessions*, Book II, Chapter 1, 40.

27. See Lucy Beckett's excellent book, *In the Light of Christ: Writings in the Western Tradition* (San Francisco: Ignatius, 2006), especially her two chapters of commentary and historical context regarding Augustine, the first on *Confessions* and the second on *The City of God*, 83–129.

28. Ephesians 4:1, 2; Romans 8:29.

Chapter 4

1. Lewis B. Smedes Quotes, "Discernment," https://www.allgreatquotes.com/quote-251817/; Center for the Advancement of Well-being, "Famous Quotes on Discernment and Well-being," George Mason University, https://wellbeing.gmu.edu/articles/11873.

2. Second Life is a massive multi-player online role-playing game. See https://secondlife.com/.

3. Sherry Turkle, *Alone Together: Why We Expect More from Technology and Less from Each Other* (New York: Basic, 2011), 1.

4. Henri J. M. Nouwen, *Reaching Out: The Three Movements of the Spiritual Life* (New York: Image, 1986), 71.

5. See Jim Wallis, *The (Un)Common Good: How the Gospel Brings Hope to a World Divided* (Grand Rapids: Brazos, 2014).

6. Quoted in Tissa Balasuriya, *The Eucharist and Human Liberation* (Eugene: Wipf & Stock, 2004), 26.

7. Clifford G. Christians, "Evangelical Perspectives on Technology," *Evangelical Christians and Popular Culture*, vol. 1, ed. Robert H. Woods Jr. (Santa Barbara: Praeger, 2013), 323. Ross Douthat of the *New York Times* in his piece "The Culture of Narcissism" notes that this portrait is at odds with the common assumption that today's youth are "more idealistic, more civic-minded, and more engaged with the world than [their] cynical Gen X predecessors," 2010, https://douthat.blogs.nytimes.com/2010/06/02/the-culture-of-narcissism/, para 5.

8. Quoted in Richard Covington, "The Salon Interview: David Mamet," *Salon*, October 24 (1997), para. 20.

9. Nathan Foster, *The Making of an Ordinary Saint* (Grand Rapids: Baker, 2014), 16.

10. Jeanne Guyon, *Union with God*, Library of Spiritual Classics, vol. 3 (Sargent: The Seedsowers, 1999), 48.

11. Quoted in Elisabeth Elliot, *Through Gates of Splendor* (New York: Harper & Brothers, 1957), 20.

12. Leonard Sweet, *Nudge: Awakening Each Other to the God Who's Already There* (Colorado Springs: David C. Cook, 2010), 105.

13. See Robert H. Woods Jr., and Paul D. Patton, *Prophetically Incorrect: A Christian Introduction to Media Criticism* (Grand Rapids: Brazos, 2010), chapter 6.

14. Flannery O'Connor, *Collected Works* (New York: Library of America, 1988), 949. Thanks to Christina Bieber and her work, which pointed us to the quote from O'Connor.

15. Charles Taylor, *Sources of the Self: The Making of Modern Identity* (Cambridge: Harvard University Press, 1989), 98.

16. See Frederick Hartt, *Art: A History of Painting, Sculpture, Architecture*, vol. 2 (Englewood Cliffs: Prentice-Hall, 1976), 317; Wolfgang Kayser, *The Grotesque in Art and Literature*, trans. Ulrich Weisstein (Bloomington: Indiana University Press, 1963); Wolfgang Stechow, "Hieronymus Bosch: The Grotesque and We," in *The Grotesque in Art and Literature: Theological Reflections*, ed. James Luther Adams and Wilson Yates (Grand Rapids: Eerdmans, 1997), 113–24.

17. Peter Gabriel, "Big Time" [Album: *So*] (Santa Monica: Geffen Records, 1986).

18. See 1 Kings 19:1–18.

Chapter 5

1. Hans Fantel, *William Penn: Apostle of Dissent* (New York: William Morrow and Company, 1974), 105.

2. Clive Thompson, "Your Outboard Brain Knows All," *Wired*, September 25, 2007, http://www.wired.com/2007/09/st-thompson-3/, para 8.

3. Sacred interiority is something we can develop over time to help thwart the unhealthy elements of mass media and "mass-minding" saturation. Mass-minding is a process that shapes the contours of what the imagination assumes is possible and what the mind asserts as normal. This chapter suggests that the dilemma of media saturation

is not only associated with the prevalence of media accessibility (the close proximity of the dance floor) and the increasing narrative efficiency of programming to insure dance participants more scintillating dances and dance partners, but also associated with the lack of a balancing, robust, and sacred interior life.

4. See also Psalm 119:11 and Jeremiah 31:33, which reinforce this key idea in slightly different language.

5. Nicholas Carr, "Is Google Making Us Stupid?", *The Atlantic*, July/August 2008, http://www.theatlantic.com/magazine/archive/2008/07/is-google-making-us-stupid/306868/, para. 9.

6. Rakefet Ackerman and Morris Goldsmith, "Metacognitive Regulation of Text Learning: On Screen versus on Paper," *Journal of Experimental Psychology: Applied* 17, no. 1 (2011): 18–32. As Ferris Jabr explains, in more than 100 studies since the 1980s, researchers in several fields have studied how our brains respond differently to onscreen text than text on paper. Before the early 1990s most of the research concluded that people read more slowly, less accurately, and less comprehensively on screens than on paper. Studies published since the early 1990s, however, have produced more inconsistent results: "A slight majority has confirmed earlier conclusions, but almost as many have found few significant differences in reading speed or comprehension between paper and screens. And recent surveys suggest that although most people still prefer paper—especially when reading intensively—attitudes are changing as tablets and e-reading technology improve and reading digital books for facts and fun becomes more common. In the U.S., e-books currently make up between 15 and 20 percent of all trade book sales" (para. 5). Ferris Jabr, "The Reading Brain in the Digital Age: The Science of Paper versus Screens," *Scientific American*, April 11, 2013, https://www.scientificamerican.com/article/reading-paper-screens/.

7. Nicholas Carr, *The Shallows: What the Internet Is Doing to Our Brains* (New York: W.W. Norton, 2010), 7.

8. See Alice Bell, "Memory in the Digital Age," *The Guardian*, January 13, 2012, http://www.theguardian.com/lifeandstyle/2012/jan/14/memories-in-the-digital-age; and Carolyn Gregoire, "How Technology Is Warping Your Memory," *Huffington Post*, December 6, 2017, http://www.huffingtonpost.com/2013/12/11/technology-changes-memory_n_4414778.html.

9. Linda A. Henkel, "Point-and-Shoot Memories: The Influence of Taking Photos on Memory for a Museum Tour," *Psychological Sciences* 25, no. 2 (2014): 396–402.

10. Evgeny Morozov, *To Save Everything, Click Here: The Folly of Technological Solutionism* (New York: Public Affairs, 2013), 277–78.

11. Multiple studies show the Internet has the potential to increase our speed of information processing and visual attention. One study of 6,442 people between ages 50 and 89 found that being "digitally literate" helps reduce the side-effects of aging on memory and may even lower rates for such maladies as dementia over time. See André J. Xavier, Eleonora d'Orsi, Cesar M. de Oliveira, Martin Orrell, Panayotes Demakakos, Jane P. Biddulph, and Michael G. Marmot, "English Longitudinal Study of Aging: Can Internet/E-mail Use Reduce Cognitive Decline?" *The Journals of Gerontology: Series A* 69, no. 9 (2014): 1117–21.

12. According to Donald W. Shriver, such instrumental values act tyrannically as "a spiritual guillotine, decapitating other values" that have cultural and transcendent staying power ("Man and His Machines: Four Angels of Vision," *Technology and Culture* 13 [October 1972]: 537). A society committed to instrumental values "eliminates all moral

obstructions to their ascendency," says Clifford G. Christians in *Good News: Social Ethics and the Press* (New York: Oxford University Press, 1993): 171—just as in ancient days people would "put out the eyes of nightingales in order to make them sing better" (Jacques Ellul, *Presence of the Kingdom* [1948; reprint, New York: Seabury, 1967], 75).

13. C. S. Lewis, *The Abolition of Man* (New York: HarperCollins, 1941), 77.

14. Rumi, "Praising Manner," trans. Coleman Barks, in *The Winged Energy of Delight: Selected Translations*, ed. by Robert Bly (New York: Perennial, 2005), 342.

15. Emily Dickinson, "Poem no. 254," in *The Complete Poems of Emily Dickinson*, ed. Thomas H. Johnson (New York: Back Bay, 1976), 116.

16. When tempted by sinful habits or distractions, we will inevitably call something "to mind." Of course, it will be radically different depending upon whether we are yielding to the temptation or not. For instance, in yielding to the temptation, what the mind explains through the instrument of conscience is that "no one will be hurt," or "I'm only human," or even something like, "I deserve it and she doesn't!" Generally, what is called to mind during sinful choices is some form of self-justification. In other words, the assertion "called to mind" provides context and rationale for our choices and our story.

On the other hand, in resisting temptation—and one reason it is called temptation is because it *is* tempting—we are hopefully in the habit of calling something "to mind," like Christ in the wilderness or Paul's reminder that "no temptation has overtaken you except what is common to mankind" (1 Cor. 10:13a, NIV). Both Jesus and his Apostle Paul were cognitively, mentally, drawing on overarching certainties that contextualized their temptation, reminding them (and us) of victorious truths and God's ultimate provision.

17. Quoted in Ralph M. Novak Jr., *Christianity and the Roman Empire* (Harrisburg: Trinity Press International, 2001), 46.

18. Jonathan Edwards, *Freedom of the Will*, Part II, sec. 9, (1754; reprint, CreateSpace, 2013), 52.

Chapter 6

1. Abraham Joshua Heschel, *Man Is Not Alone: A Philosophy of Religion* (New York: Harper and Row, 1966), 78.

2. John Calvin, *Golden Booklet of the True Christian Life*, trans. by Henry J. Van Andel (Grand Rapids: Baker, 1952), 20.

3. Keith R. Anderson, *A Spirituality of Listening: Living What We Hear* (Downer's Grove, IL: IVP Books), 110.

4. Most readers pause a minute when they read this one since it seems counterproductive. This option, however, can lead to gratitude for the many blessings God has brought about from that rejection or apparent failure and help re-focus your thinking about your life's vocation. One of your authors (Paul) framed the rejection letter he received in response to his application for the college he taught at some forty years later. Your other author (Robert) regularly re-visits rejection letters from journal editors. The articles, later published in other journals, were much better than the original submissions. In both cases, these rejections led to redemptive acts that now, with the benefit of hindsight and the wisdom of God's guiding hand, inspire us toward more leaps of creative and professional faith in all areas of life.

5. See Howard Snyder, *Populist Saints: B. T. and Ellen Roberts and the First Free Methodists* (Grand Rapids: Eerdmans, 2006), 27.

6. Martin Luther, "Essentials of the Bible," quoted in *Faith Alone: A Daily Devotional*, ed. by James C. Galvin (Grand Rapids: Zondervan, 2005), November 6.

7. J. R. R. Tolkien, *The Fellowship of the Ring: Being the First Part of the Lord of the Rings* (New York: Ballantine, 1954), 55–56.

8. Irenaeus, *Against Heresies*, IV, 21, vol. 1, *The Ante-Nicene Fathers*, ed. by Alexander Roberts and James Donaldson (reprint, New York: Charles Scribner's Sons, 1899), 493.

9. E. Stanley Jones, in his book *Conversion*, quoted in *Devotional Classics: Selected Readings for Individuals and Groups*, ed. by Richard J. Foster and James Bryan Smith (San Francisco: HarperCollins, 1993), 303.

10. Quentin J. Schultze, *Habits of the High-Tech Heart: Living Virtuously in the Information Age* (Grand Rapids: Baker Academic, 2002), 75. See also G. K. Chesterton, *Orthodoxy: The Romance of Faith* (New York: Image, 1990), 48.

11. Neil Postman, *Technopoly: The Surrender of Culture to Technology* (New York: Vintage, 1992).

12. See Google, "Google's Mission," https://www.google.com/about/company/.

13. Siva Vaidhyanathan, *The Googlization of Everything (And Why We Should Worry)* (Berkeley: University of California Press, 2011), 13.

14. Schultze, *Habits of the High-Tech Heart*, 21.

15. "Alternative consciousness" is a phrase that comes from Walter Brueggemann, *Prophetic Imagination*, 2nd ed. (Minneapolis: Fortress, 2001), 13.

16. For a discussion of this and other Ignatian theology, see David L. Fleming, S.J., *The Spiritual Exercises of St. Ignatius: A Literal Translation and Contemporary Reading* (St. Louis: St. Louis Institute of Jesuit Sources, 1978).

Chapter 7

1. Nina Mandell, "Ronda Rousey Said She Thought About Committing Suicide Shortly After Her Loss to Holly Holm," *USA Today Sports*, February 16, 2016, http://mmajunkie.com/2016/02/ronda-rousey-tells-ellen-degeneres-she-thought-about-suicide-after-loss-to-holly-holm/, para. 4.

2. Author and researcher Sherry Turkle asserts that the social mediated "collaborative self" is pulling participants away from the non-digital personal encounter by social media's ability to lessen the risk of verbal and non-verbal initiatives. Tweets can be contoured; conversations on Gchat can avoid the vulnerability of being "too emotional." See Turkle's book *Reclaiming Conversation: The Power of Talk in a Digital Age* (New York: Penguin, 2015), 34.

3. Francis de Sales, "Letter of June 1607," in *Francis de Sales, Jane de Chantal: Letters of Spiritual Direction*, trans. Péronne Marie Thibert (New York: Paulist, 1988), 112: "Don't sow your desires in someone else's garden; just cultivate your own as best you can. . . . What is the use of building castles in Spain since we have to live in France? This is my old lesson, . . . ".

4. Su Holmes, "It's a Jungle Out There!: Playing the Game of Fame in Celebrity Reality TV," Su Holmes and Sean Redmond, eds., *Framing Celebrity* (New York: Routledge, 2006), 47.

5. We are deeply indebted to our friend and mentor, pilot, island owner, log cabin builder, former Wheaton College professor, and all-around good egg Emory (Em) Griffin and his celebrated book *A First Look at Communication Theory*, now in its tenth

edition (New York: McGraw-Hill, 2019) for introducing us to Kenneth Burke's Dramatism Theory during graduate school. Much of our thinking about the characteristics of hierarchy derives from Burke's work.

6. Kenneth Burke, *Language as Symbolic Action: Essays on Life, Literature and Method* (Los Angeles: University of California Press, 1966), 16.

7. Richard Hornsby, *The End of Acting: A Radical View* (New York: Applause Theatre, 1992), 17.

8. Thomas De Zengotita, *Mediated: How the Media Shapes Your World and the Way You Live in It* (New York: Bloomsbury, 2005), 11.

9. Christopher Lasch, *The Culture of Narcissism: American Life in an Age of Diminishing Expectations* (New York: Norton, 1991), 21.

10. See Jean M. Twenge, Keith W. Campbell, and Elise C. Freeman, "Generational Differences in Young Adults' Life Goals, Concern for Others, and Civic Orientation, 1966–2009," *Journal of Personality and Social Psychology* 102, no. 5 (2012): 1045–62, and Jean M. Twenge, *Generation Me: Why Today's Young Americans Are More Confident, Assertive, Entitled—and More Miserable Than Ever Before*, rev. and upd. (New York: Atria, 2014).

11. Orville Gilbert Brim, *Look at Me!: The Fame Motive from Childhood to Death* (Ann Arbor: University of Michigan Press, 2009). See also Elizabeth Landau, "How the 'Fame Motive' Makes You Want to Be a Star," *CNN*, October 28, 2009, http://www.cnn.com/2009/HEALTH/10/28/psychology.fame.celebrity/, para. 21.

12. See Famous for a Day, https://famousforaday.co/about/index.html.

13. Landau, "How the 'Fame Motive' Makes You Want to Be a Star," para. 29. See also Brim, *Look at Me!*

14. For a humorous take on how Twitter shapes your self-identiy, see Ben Walker, "The Twitter Song," http://music.ihatemornings.com/track/youre-no-one-if-youre-not-on-twitter.Ben also has a blog, ihatemornings.com.

15. This somewhat hilariously absurd argument among the disciples of Jesus as to which of them would be "the greatest" should be a helpful reminder for anyone discouraged with outcomes. For your authors, that might be discouragement about student outcomes or student evaluations in our courses. Here are the disciples of Christ, having witnessed the power of his teaching and miracles, arguing about their own future significance. It is an important example of the human propensity to "miss the point."

16. W. L. Sheldon, "What to Believe: An Ethical Creed," in *Ethical Addresses*, Series 4, No. 4 (Philadelphia: S. Burns Weston, 1897), 61.

Chapter 8

1. D. F. Payne, "Face," in *The Illustrated Bible Dictionary: Aaron-Golan*, Part 1, ed. J. D. Douglas (Downers Grove: InterVarsity Press, 1980), 496. See also Numbers 6:24–26.

2. Chris Hedges, *Empire of Illusion: The End of Literacy and the Triumph of Spectacle* (New York: Nation, 2009), 17.

3. In Matthew 5:43–48, Jesus commands us to "be perfect, therefore, as your heavenly Father is perfect" and to "love your enemies" as your participation by grace in the impartiality of God (NIV). We mortals are "perfect" as we shine and share His provisions indiscriminately. By grace, we gain the wisdom and power of His presence through loving service even to those who defiantly disregard Him. The sun and rain, components necessary for the existence of humanity, manifest God's indiscriminate,

loving care for His creation. Jesus tells his followers that their lives are to be similarly virtuous and non-discriminating.

4. Two brief caveats are in order at this point. First, God's indiscriminate grace shining on the good as well as the evil does not obliterate the principle of sowing and reaping, cause and effect (Gal. 6:7). Grace is bestowed upon the righteous as well as the unrighteous. Second, the biblical emphasis on impartiality does not obliterate the value of hierarchical structures in every civilization. Jesus told his followers that the Pharisees and teachers of the Law sat "in Moses' seat," and because of this positional authority as guides, they should be obeyed: "So you must be careful to do everything they tell you. But do not do what they do, for they do not practice what they preach" (Matt. 23:2–3, NIV). Such hypocrisy, detailed in the "Seven Woes Discourse" of Matthew 23:13–39, does not disavow the practical necessity of authority and submission to authority. For instance, the Apostle Paul repented after verbally assaulting the high priest, Ananias, who had just ordered Paul to be struck on the mouth. After calling Ananias a "white-washed wall," and asserting "God will strike you" for disregarding the Jewish law concerning punishment of the accused, Paul is informed that he is verbally attacking the high priest. He then confesses, "Brothers, I did not realize that he was the high priest; for it is written: 'Do not speak evil about the ruler of your people'" (Acts 23:1–5, NIV). Paul's confession before the Sanhedrin referenced the Jewish law's emphasis on respectful recognition of ecclesiastical and political authority (Exod. 22:28). Even if the Apostle Paul felt the Temple guard unjustly struck him, to him the high priest of Israel was still the high priest. Students, then, must respect the positional authority of teachers and directors, just as artistic novices should accept the tacit authority of masters.

5. Francis de Sales, "Letter of June 1607," in *Francis de Sales, Jane de Chantal: Letters of Spiritual Direction*, trans. Péronne Marie Thibert (New York: Paulist, 1988), 112.

6. Even the difficult rite of passage known to millions as the mid-life crisis can be understood as despondency over one's place along the success ladder, a despair and discontentedness related to the grievous falling short of aspirations launched at the beginning of the career path.

7. Gregory H. Spencer, *Awakening the Quieter Virtues* (Downers Grove: IVP, 2010), 11.

8. Vincent J. Miller, *Consuming Religion: Christian Faith and Practice in a Consumer Culture* (New York: Continuum, 2003), 193.

9. Augustine, *On Christian Teaching*, trans. R. P. H. Green (New York: Oxford University Press, 1997), 9.

10. Abraham Joshua Heschel, *Moral Grandeur and Spiritual Audacity* (New York: Farrar, Straus and Giroux, 1996), 92.

11. Thomas Aquinas qtd. in James Weisheipl and Fabian R. Larcher, trans., *Commentary on the Gospel of John*, Aquinas Scripture Series, 4 (Albany: Magi, 1980), 242.

12. Augustine, *On Christian Teaching*, 9. See also Colossians 3:1–5.

13. Spencer, *Awakening the Quieter Virtues*, 150–151.

14. Ibid., 152.

Chapter 9

1. Blaise Pascal, *Pensées*, ed. and trans. Roger Ariew (Indianapolis: Hackett, 2004), 38.

2. We highly recommend Peter Kreeft's helpful commentary on Pascal's classic, *Christianity for Modern Pagans: Pascal's Pensées, Edited, Outlined, and Explained* (San Francisco: Ignatius, 1993). See especially chapter 13, "Diversions."

3. Thomas Merton, *Faith and Violence: Christian Teaching and Christian Practice* (South Bend: University of Notre Dame Press, 1968), 150.

4. Cornell West, *Prophetic Thought in Postmodern Times* (Monroe: Common Courage, 1993), 6.

5. This "Allegiance Prayer" is from Direction for Our Times, https://direction forourtimes.com/prayer-guide/.

6. Abraham Joshua Heschel, *God in Search of Man: A Philosophy of Judaism* (New York: Harper and Row, 1955), 74.

7. Walter Brueggemann, *Sabbath as Resistance: Saying No to the Culture of Now* (Louisville: Westminster John Knox, 2014), 20–21.

8. Charles H. Spurgeon, *Morning and Evening: A Devotional Classic for Daily Encouragement*, 2nd ed. (Boston: Hendrickson, 1991), 203.

9. Thomas à Kempis, *Of the Imitation of Christ*, trans. Ronald Knox and Michael Oakley (Westwood: Revell, 1968), 18.

10. Quentin J. Schultze, *Habits of the High-Tech Heart: Living Virtuously in the Information Age* (Grand Rapids: Baker Academic, 2002), 26.

Bibliography

Ackerman, Rakefet, and Morris Goldsmith. "Metacognitive Regulation of Text Learning: On Screen versus on Paper." *Journal of Experimental Psychology: Applied 17*, no. 1 (2011): 18–32.

"Allegiance Prayer." Direction for Our Times. https://directionforourtimes.com/prayer-guide/.

American Optometric Association. "Survey Reveals Parents Drastically Underestimate the Time Kids Spend on Electronic Devices." *Cision PR Newswire*, July 22, 2014. https://www.prnewswire.com/news-releases/survey-reveals-parents-drastically-underestimate-the-time-kids-spend-on-electronic-devices-268088521.html.

Anderson, Keith. *A Spirituality of Listening: Living What We Hear* (Downers Grove: IVP Books, 2016), 110.

Ankerberg, John, and Dillon Burroughs. *What Can Be Found in "LOST": Insights on God and the Meaning of Life*. Eugene: Harvest House, 2008.

Aquinas, Thomas. *Commentary on the Gospel of John*. Translated by James Weisheipl and Fabian R. Larcher. Aquinas Scripture Series 4. Albany: Magi, 1980.

Augustine. *On Christian Teaching*. Translated by R. P. H. Green. New York: Oxford University Press, 1997.

——. *The Confessions of Saint Augustine*. Book II, Chapter 1. Translated by Rex Warner. New York: Mentor-Omega, 1963.

——. *The Confessions of Saint Augustine*. Book III, Chapter 3. Translated by Rex Warner. New York: Mentor-Omega, 1963.

——. *The Confessions of Saint Augustine*. Book X, Chapter 8. Translated by Rex Warner. New York: Mentor-Omega, 1963.

Balasuriya, Tissa. *The Eucharist and Human Liberation*. Eugene: Wipf & Stock, 2004.

Barna Research Group. "How Technology is Changing Millennial Faith." October 15, 2013. https://www.barna.com/research/how-technology-is-changing-millenial-faith/.

Beckett, Lucy. *In the Light of Christ: Writings in the Western Tradition*. San Francisco: Ignatius, 2006.

Bell, Alice. "Memory in the Digital Age." *The Guardian*, December 6, 2017. https://www.theguardian.com/lifeandstyle/2012/jan/14/memories-in-the-digital-age.

Brim, Orville Gilbert. *Look at Me! The Fame Motive from Childhood to Death*. Ann Arbor: University of Michigan Press, 2009.

Brueggemann, Walter. *Prophetic Imagination*. 2nd ed. Minneapolis: Fortress, 2001.

——. *Sabbath as Resistance: Saying No to the Culture of Now.* Louisville: Westminster John Knox, 2014.

Bruner, Kurt, and Jim Ware. *Finding God in the Lord of the Rings.* Carol Stream: Tyndale, 2006.

Burke, Kenneth. *Language as Symbolic Action: Essays on Life, Literature and Method.* Los Angeles: University of California Press, 1966.

Calvin, John. *Golden Booklet of the True Christian Life.* Translated by Henry J. Van Andel. Grand Rapids: Baker, 1952.

Carr, Nicholas. "Is Google Making Us Stupid?" *The Atlantic*, July/August 2008. http://www.theatlantic.com/magazine/archive/2008/07/is-google-making-us-stupid/306868/.

——. *The Shallows: What the Internet Is Doing to Our Brains.* New York: W.W. Norton, 2010.

Center for the Advancement of Well-being. "Famous Quotes on Discernment and Well-being." George Mason University. https://wellbeing.gmu.edu/articles/11873.

Chambers, Oswald. "The Spiritually Vigorous Saint." In *My Utmost for His Highest.* July 11. https://utmost.org/the-spiritually-vigorous-saint/.

——. "Shallow and Profound." In *My Utmost for His Highest.* November 22. https://utmost.org/shallow-and-profound/.

Chesterton, G. K. *Orthodoxy: The Romance of Faith.* New York: Image, 1990.

Christians, Clifford G. "Evangelical Perspectives on Technology." In Vol. 1, *Evangelical Christians and Popular Culture*, edited by Robert H. Woods Jr., 323-340. Santa Barbara: Praeger, 2013.

——. *Good News: Social Ethics and the Press.* New York: Oxford University Press, 1993.

Cooper, Thomas W. *Fast Media, Media Fast: How to Clear Your Mind and Invigorate Your Life in an Age of Media Overload.* Boulder: Gaeta, 2011.

Covington, Richard. "The Salon Interview: David Mamet." *Salon*, October 24, 1997.

Crouch, Andy. "The Joyful Environmentalists: Eugene Peterson and Peter Harris Think of Creation Care Not as An Onerous Duty but a Natural Response to the Goodness of God." *Christianity Today* 55, no. 6 (2011): 30–32.

Culkin, John M., S.J. "A Schoolman's Guide to Marshall McLuhan." *The Saturday Review*, March 18, 1967. https://www.unz.com/print/SaturdayRev-1967mar18-00051.

Danesi, Marcel. *Popular Culture: Introductory Perspectives.* Lanham: Rowman and Littlefield, 2008.

Dark, David. *Everyday Apocalypse: The Sacred Revealed in Radiohead, The Simpsons, and Other Pop Culture Icons.* Grand Rapids: Brazos, 2002.

Detweiler, Craig. *Selfies: Searching for the Image of God in a Digital Age.* Grand Rapids: Brazos, 2018.

Detweiler, Craig, and Barry Taylor. *A Matrix of Meanings: Finding God in Pop Culture.* Grand Rapids: Baker, 2003.

Dickinson, Emily "Poem no. 254." In *The Complete Poems of Emily Dickinson*, edited by Thomas H. Johnson, 116. New York: Back Bay, 1976.

Douthat, Ross. "The Culture of Narcissism." *The New York Times*, June 2, 2010. https://douthat.blogs.nytimes.com/2010/06/02/the-culture-of-narcissism/.

Dreher, Rod. *The Benedict Option: A Strategy for Christians in a Post-Christian Nation.* New York: Sentinel, 2017.

Dye, John. "Pope Francis Calls Texts, Internet, Social Media 'Gifts of God,'" *Android Authority*, January 22, 2016. http://www.androidauthority.com/pope-internet-gift-god-669125/.

Earl, Jennifer. "Dad Creates App That Freezes Your Kids' Phones Until They Answer Your Texts." *CBS News*, August 23, 2017. https://www.cbsnews.com/news/this-dad-created-an-app-that-freezes-your-kids-phones-until-they-answer-your-texts/.

Edwards, Jonathan. *Freedom of the Will*. Part II. Section. 9. 1754. Reprint. CreateSpace, 2013.

Elliot, Elisabeth. *Through Gates of Splendor*. New York: Harper & Brothers, 1957.

Ellul, Jacques. *Presence of the Kingdom*, 1948; Reprint, New York: Seabury, 1967.

Elpidorou, Andreas. "The Bright Side of Boredom." *Frontiers in Psychology*, November 3, 2014. https://www.frontiersin.org/articles/10.3389/fpsyg.2014.01245/.

Famous for a Day. https://famousforaday.co/about/index.html.

Fantel, Hans. *William Penn: Apostle of Dissent*. New York: William Morrow, 1974.

Fleming, David L., S.J. *The Spiritual Exercises of St. Ignatius: A Literal Translation and Contemporary Reading*. St. Louis: St. Louis Institute of Jesuit Sources, 1978.

Foster, Nathan. *The Making of an Ordinary Saint*. Grand Rapids: Baker, 2014.

Foster, Richard J. *Celebration of Discipline: The Path to Spiritual Growth*. New York: Harper One, 1998.

Foster, Richard J., and James Bryan Smith, eds. *Devotional Classics: Selected Readings for Individuals and Groups*, 19–23. San Francisco: Harper Collins, 1993.

Gabriel, Peter. "*Big Time*." Album: *So*. Santa Monica: Geffen Records, 1986.

Garfield, Bob. "The Persuaders." *Frontline*, November 9, 2004. https://www.pbs.org/wgbh/pages/frontline/shows/persuaders/etc/script.html.

Garling, Caleb. "Snapchat Could Capitalize on Users' Undivided Attention." *SFGATE*, December 11, 2013. http://www.sfgate.com/technology/article/Snapchat-could-capitalize-on-users-undivided-5056295.php.

Godawa, Brian. *Hollywood Worldviews: Watching Films with Wisdom and Discernment*. Downers Grove: InterVarsity, 2002.

Google, "Google's Mission." https://about.google/.

Greeley, Andrew M. *God in Popular Culture*. Chicago: Thomas More, 1989.

Gregoire, Carolyn. "How Technology is Warping your Mind." *The Huffington Post*, December 6, 2017. https://www.huffpost.com/entry/technology-changes-memory_n_4414778.

Griffin, Emory, Andrew Ledbetter, and Glen Sparks. *A First Look at Communication Theory*. 10th ed. New York: McGraw-Hill, 2014.

Guyon, Jeanne. *Union with God*, Library of Spiritual Classics, vol. 3. Sargent: The Seedsowers, 1999.

Hartt, Frederick. *Art: A History of Painting, Sculpture, Architecture*, vol. 2. Englewood Cliffs: Prentice-Hall, 1976.

Hedges, Chris. *Empire of Illusion: The End of Literacy and the Triumph of Spectacle*. New York: Nation, 2009.

Henkel, Linda A. "Point-and-Shoot Memories: The Influence of Taking Photos on Memory for a Museum Tour." *Psychological Sciences* 25, no. 2 (2014): 396–402.

Heschel, Abraham Joshua. *I Asked for Wonder: A Spiritual Anthology*. New York: Crossway, 1983.

——. *God in Search of Man: A Philosophy of Judaism*. New York: Harper and Row, 1955.

——. *Man Is Not Alone: A Philosophy of Religion*. New York: Harper and Row, 1966.

———. *Moral Grandeur and Spiritual Audacity*. New York: Farrar, Straus and Giroux, 1996.

Holmes, Su. "It's a Jungle Out There!: Playing the Game of Fame in Celebrity Reality TV." In *Framing Celebrity*, edited by Su Holmes and Sean Redmond, 45–66. New York: Routledge, 2006.

Hornsby, Richard. *The End of Acting: A Radical View*. New York: Applause Theatre, 1992.

Huth, Alexander G., et al. "Natural Speech Reveals the Semantic Maps That Tile Human Cerebral Cortex." *Nature: International Journal of Science* 532 (April 2016): 453–58.

Irenaeus. *Against Heresies*, IV, 21. In Vol. 1, *The Ante-Nicene Fathers*, edited by Alexander Roberts and James Donaldson, 492–93. Reprint. New York: Charles Scribner's Sons, 1899.

Jabr, Ferris. "The Reading Brain in the Digital Age: The Science of Paper versus Screens." *Scientific American*, April 11, 2013. https://www.scientificamerican.com/article/reading-paper-screens/.

Jones, E. Stanley. *Abundant Living*. New York: Abingdon-Cokesbury, 1947.

Kayser, Wolfgang. *The Grotesque in Art and Literature*. Translated by Ulrich Weisstein. Bloomington: Indiana University Press, 1963.

Keller, Timothy. *The Prodigal God: Recovering the Heart of the Christian Faith*. New York: Riverhead, 2008.

Kempis, Thomas à. *Of the Imitation of Christ*. Translated by Ronald Knox and Michael Oakley. Westwood: Revell, 1968.

Kimball, Roger. "What Did Kierkegaard Want?" *New Criterion*, September 2001. http://www.newcriterion.com/articles.cfm/What-did-Kierkegaard-want---2132.

Kreeft, Peter. *Christianity for Modern Pagans: Pascal's Pensées, Edited, Outlined, and Explained*. San Francisco: Ignatius, 1993.

Kuyper, Abraham. "Modernism: A Fata Morgana in the Christian Domain." In *Abraham Kuyper: A Centennial Reader*, edited by James D. Bratt, 87–124. Grand Rapids: Eerdmans, 1998.

Lally, Phillippa, et al. "How Are Habits Formed: Modelling Habit Formation in the Real World." *European Journal of Social Psychology* 40, no. 6 (2010): 998–1009.

Landau, Elizabeth. "How the 'Fame Motive' Makes You Want to Be a Star." *CNN*, October 28, 2009. http://www.cnn.com/2009/HEALTH/10/28/psychology.fame.celebrity/.

Lasch, Christopher. *The Culture of Narcissism: American Life in an Age of Diminishing Expectations*. New York: Norton, 1991.

Lewis, C. S. *The Abolition of Man*. New York: HarperCollins, 1941.

———. "Christian Apologetics." In *God in the Dock: Essays on Theology and Ethics*, edited by Walter Hooper, 89–103. Grand Rapids: Eerdmans, 1994.

———. *Screwtape Letters*. 1942; Reprint. New York: HarperCollins, 2001.

Lewis, Paul. "'Our Minds Can Be Hijacked': The Tech Insiders Who Fear a Smartphone Dystopia." *OSHO News*, November 7, 2017. https://www.theguardian.com/technology/2017/oct/05/smartphone-addiction-silicon-valley-dystopia.

Locke, John. *An Essay Concerning Human Understanding*. Book 2, 19 (1689. Reprint). Greensboro: WLC, 2009.

Loh, Kep Kee, and Ryota Kanai. "How Has the Internet Reshaped Human Cognition?" *The Neuroscientist* 22, no. 5 (2016): 506–20.

Luther, Martin. "Essentials of the Bible." In *Faith Alone: A Daily Devotional*, edited by James C. Galvin (Grand Rapids: Zondervan, 2005), November 6.

McLuhan, Marshall. *Understanding Media: The Extensions of Man*. New York: McGraw-Hill, 1964.

MacDonald, Gordon. "God's Calling Plan: So, What Exactly Is a Call to Ministry?" *ctpastors*, 2003. http://www.christianitytoday.com/pastors/2003/fall/3.35.html.

Mandell, Nina. "Ronda Rousey Said She Thought About Committing Suicide Shortly After Her Loss to Holly Holm." *USA Today Sports*, February 16, 2016. http://mmajunkie.com/2016/02/ronda-rousey-tells-ellen-degeneres-she-thought-about-suicide-after-loss-to-holly-holm/.

Media Ecology Association. http//media-ecology.org/about-us/.

Menzie, Nicola. "Heartpoints App Helps Christians Track How Well or Wobbly They Walk with the Lord." *The Christian Post*, September 2, 2013. https://www.christianpost.com/news/heartpoints-app-helps-christians-track-how-well-or-wobbly-they-walk-with-the-lord.html.

Merton, Thomas. *Faith and Violence: Christian Teaching and Christian Practice*. South Bend: University of Notre Dame Press, 1968.

Miller, Vincent J. *Consuming Religion: Christian Faith and Practice in a Consumer Culture*. New York: Continuum, 2003.

Moore, Charles E., ed. *Provocations: Spiritual Writings of Kierkegaard*. Farmington: Plough, 2002.

Morozov, Evgeny. *To Save Everything, Click Here: The Folly of Technological Solutionism*. New York: Public Affairs, 2013.

Myers, Kenneth A. *All God's Children and Blue Suede Shoes: Christians and Popular Culture*. Wheaton, IL: Crossway, 1989.

Nicholi, Armand. *The Question of God: C. S. Lewis and Sigmund Freud Debate God, Love, Sex, and the Meaning of Life*. New York: Free, 2003.

Nouwen, Henri J. M. *Reaching Out: The Three Movements of the Spiritual Life*. New York: Image, 1986.

Novak Jr., Ralph M. *Christianity and the Roman Empire*. Harrisburg: Trinity Press International, 2001.

O'Connor, Flannery. *Collected Works*. New York: Library of America, 1988.

Oden, Thomas C. *After Modernity . . . What?* Grand Rapids: Zondervan, 1992.

Ong, Walter. *Orality and Literacy: The Technologizing of the Word*. New York: Routledge, 1982.

Parker, Dorothy, and Ellen Parr. "The Cure for Boredom Is Curiosity. There Is No Cure for Curiosity." *Quote Investigator*. https://quoteinvestigator.com/2015/11/01/cure/.

Pascal, Blaise. *Pensées*. Translated by A.J. Krailsheimer. Harmondsworth, England: Penguin, 1986.

——. *Pensées*. Edited and translated by Roger Ariew. Indianapolis: Hackett, 2004.

Pauley, John L. and Amy King. "Evangelicals' Passion for *The Passion of the Christ*." In Vol. 1, *Evangelical Christians and Popular Culture: Pop Goes the Gospel*, edited by Robert H. Woods Jr., 36–51. Santa Barbara: Praeger.

Payne, D. F. "Face." In *The Illustrated Bible Dictionary: Aaron-Golan*, Part 1, 495–96, edited by J. D. Douglas. Downers Grove: InterVarsity Press, 1980.

Peterson, Eugene. *The Pastor: A Memoir*. New York: HarperCollins, 2012.

Piatt, Christian. *"LOST": A Search for Meaning*. St. Louis: Chalice, 2006.

Postman, Neil. *Amusing Ourselves to Death: Public Discourse in the Age of Show Business*. New York: Penguin, 1985.

——. *Technopoly: The Surrender of Culture to Technology*. New York: Vintage, 1992.

Putnam, Robert T. *Bowling Alone: The Collapse and Revival of American Community*. New York: Simon and Schuster, 2001.

Rohr, Richard. *Everything Belongs: The Gift of Contemplative Prayer*. New York: Crossroad, 2003.

Romanowski, William D. *Eyes Wide Open: Looking for God in Popular Culture*. Rev. and exp. Grand Rapids: Brazos, 2007.

———. *Pop Culture Wars: Religion and the Role of Entertainment in American Life*. Downers Grove: InterVarsity, 1996.

Rumi. "Praising Manners." Translated by Coleman Barks. In *The Winged Energy of Delight: Selected Translations*, edited by Robert Bly, 331–48. New York: Perennial, 2005.

Sales, Francis de. "Letter of June 1607." In *Francis de Sales, Jane de Chantal: Letters of Spiritual Direction*, translated by Péronne Marie Thibert, 112–13. New York: Paulist, 1988.

Sanders, J. Oswald. *Spiritual Leadership*. Upd. and exp. Chicago: Moody, 1994.

Sawaki, Risa, Steven J. Luck, and Jane E. Raymond, "How Attention Changes in Response to Incentives." *Journal of Cognitive Neuroscience* 27, no. 11 (2015): 2229–39.

Sayers, Dorothy. *Christian Letters to a Post-Christian World: A Collection of Essays*. Grand Rapids: Eerdmans, 1969.

Schnase, Robert. "The Blessing and Curse of Ambition." *The Christian Ministry*, (January/February 1993): 16–19.

Schneider, Phil. "Christianity, There's an App for That: Heartpoints Review." *Churchmag*, September 30, 2013. https://churchm.ag/heartpoints-app-review/.

Schultze, Quentin J. *Habits of the High-Tech Heart: Living Virtuously in the Information Age*. Grand Rapids: Baker Academic, 2002.

———. *Here I Am: Now What on Earth Should I Be Doing?* Grand Rapids: Baker, 2005.

Schut, Kevin. *Of Games and God: A Christian Exploration of Video Games*. Grand Rapids: Brazos, 2013.

Seay, Chris. *The Gospel According to "LOST."* Nashville: Thomas Nelson, 2009.

Second Life. https://secondlife.com.

Sheldon, W. L. "What To Believe: An Ethical Creed." In Ethical Addresses, Series 4, No. 4, 57–76. Philadelphia: S. Burns Weston, 1897.

Shelley, Bruce. *Church History in Plain Language*, 2nd ed. Nashville: Thomas Nelson, 1995.

Shriver, Donald W. "Man and His Machines: Four Angels of Vision." *Technology and Culture* 13 (1972): 531–55.

Smedes, Lewis B. "Discernment." Lewis B. Smedes Quotes. https://www.allgreatquotes.com/quote-251817/.

Smith, James R. A. *Desiring the Kingdom: Worship, Worldview, and Cultural Formation*. Grand Rapids: Baker Academic, 2009.

———. *You Are What You Love: The Spiritual Power of Habit*. Grand Rapids: Brazos, 2016.

Snyder, Howard. *Populist Saints: B. T. and Ellen Roberts and the First Free Methodists*. Grand Rapids: Eerdmans, 2006.

Spencer, Ben. "Mobile Users Can't Leave Their Phone Alone for Six Minutes and Check It Up To 150 Times a Day." *Daily Mail.com*, February 10, 2013. http://www.dailymail.co.uk/news/article-2276752/Mobile-users-leave-phone-minutes-check-150-times-day.html.

Spencer, Gregory H. *Awakening the Quieter Virtues*. Downers Grove: IVP, 2010.

Spencer, Susan. "Driver Says GPS Led Her into Sand Trap in Northbridge." *Telegram.com*, June 20, 2012. https://www.telegram.com/article/20120620/NEWS/106209898.

Spurgeon, Charles H. *Morning and Evening: A Devotional Classic for Daily Encouragement*, 2nd ed. Boston: Hendrickson, 1991.

———. *The Treasury of David*. Vol 2. Peabody: Hendrickson, 1988.

Stechow, Wolfgang. "Hieronymus Bosch: The Grotesque and We." In *The Grotesque in Art and Literature: Theological Reflections*, edited by James Luther Adams and Wilson Yates, 113–24. Grand Rapids: Eerdmans, 1999.

Storey, John. *Cultural Theory and Popular Culture: An Introduction*, 2nd ed. New York: Routledge, 2015.

Strom, Bill. *More Than Talk: Communication Studies and the Christian Faith*, 2nd ed. Dubuque: Kendall/Hunt, 2003.

Sweet, Leonard. *Nudge: Awakening Each Other to the God Who's Already There*. Colorado Springs: David C. Cook, 2010.

Taylor, Charles. *Sources of the Self: The Making of Modern Identity*. Cambridge: Harvard University Press, 1989.

Thompson, Clive. "Your Outboard Brain Knows All." *Wired*, September 25, 2007. http://www.wired.com/2007/09/st-thompson-3/, para 8.

Tolkien, J. R. R. *The Fellowship of the Ring: Being the First Part of the Lord of the Rings*. New York: Ballantine, 1954.

Turkle, Sherry. *Alone Together: Why We Expect More from Technology and Less from Each Other*. New York: Basic, 2011.

———. *Reclaiming Conversation: The Power of Talk in a Digital Age*. New York: Penguin, 2015.

Twenge, Jean M. *Generation Me: Why Today's Young Americans Are More Confident, Assertive, Entitled—and More Miserable Than Ever Before*. Rev. and upd. New York: Atria, 2014.

Twenge, Jean M., Keith W. Campbell, and Elise C. Freeman. "Generational Differences in Young Adults' Life Goals, Concern for Others, and Civic Orientation, 1966–2009." *Journal of Personality and Social Psychology* 102, no. 5 (2012): 1045–62.

Vaidhyanathan, Siva. *The Googlization of Everything and Why We Should Worry*. Berkeley: University of California Press, 2011.

Vodanovich, Stephen J., S.J. "On the Possible Benefits of Boredom: A Neglected Area in Personality Research." *Psychology and Education: An Interdisciplinary Journal 40*, nos. 3–4 (2003): 28–33.

Walker, Ben. "I Hate Mornings." Blog. http://ihatemornings.com/.

Walker, Ben. "The Twitter Song." http://music.ihatemornings.com/track/youre-no-one-if-youre-not-on-twitter.

Wallace, David Foster. *The Pale King*. New York: Back Bay, 2011.

Wallis, Jim. *The (Un)Common Good: How the Gospel Brings Hope to a World Divided*. Grand Rapids: Brazos, 2014.

Ward, Annalee. "Themed Destinations, Museums, and Evangelicals." In Vol. 3, *Evangelical Christians and Popular Culture: Pop Goes the Gospel*, edited by Robert H. Woods Jr., 244–60. Santa Barbara: Praeger, 2013.

Weinschenk, Susan. "Why We're All Addicted to Texts, Twitter and Google." *Psychology Today*, September 11, 2012. https://www.psychologytoday.com/us/blog/brain-wise/201209/why-were-all-addicted-texts-twitter-and-google.

West, Cornell. *Prophetic Thought in Postmodern Times*. Monroe: Common Courage, 1993.

Woods Jr., Robert H., and Paul D. Patton. *Prophetically Incorrect: A Christian Introduction to Media Criticism*. Grand Rapids: Brazos, 2010.

Bibliography

Woods Jr., Robert H, et al. "Motivations for Reading the *Left Behind* Book Series: A Uses and Gratifications Analysis." *Journal of Media and Religion* 15, no. 2 (2016): 63–77.

Xavier, André J, et al. "English Longitudinal Study of Aging: Can Internet/E-mail Use Reduce Cognitive Decline?" *The Journals of Gerontology: Series A* 69, no. 9 (2014): 1117–21.

Yoffe, Emily. "Seeking: How the Brain Hard-wires Us to Love Google, Twitter, and Texting, and Why That's Dangerous." *Slate*, August 12, 2009. https://slate.com/technology/2009/08/the-powerful-and-mysterious-brain-circuitry-that-makes-us-love-google-twitter-and-texting.html.

Zengotita, Thomas De. *Mediated: How the Media Shapes Your World and the Way You Live in It*. New York: Bloomsbury, 2005.

Index

INDEX